P9-DTO-904

PS
8/96

2000
9⁹⁵

sweet basil, garlic, tomatoes,
and chives

sweet basil, garlic, tomatoes, and chives

The Vegetable Dishes of

Tuscany and Provence

Diana Shaw

Harmony Books / New York

Copyright © 1992 by Diana Shaw

All rights reserved. No part of this book may be reproduced or transmitted in any form or by any means, electronic or mechanical, including photocopying, recording, or by any information storage and retrieval system, without permission in writing from the publisher.

Published by Harmony Books, a division of Crown Publishers, Inc., 201 East 50th Street, New York, New York 10022. Member of the Crown Publishing Group.

HARMONY and colophon are trademarks of Crown Publishers, Inc.

Manufactured in the United States of America

Book design and Hand-lettering by Linda Kocur

Library of Congress Cataloging-in-Publication Data

Shaw, Diana
Sweet Basil, Garlic, Tomatoes, and Chives : the vegetable dishes of Tuscany and Provence / Diana Shaw.—1st ed.
Includes bibliographical references and index.
1. Cookery (Vegetables)   2. Cookery, French.   I. Title.
TX801.S47   1992
641.6′5′09449—dc20   91-24053
CIP

ISBN 0-517-58269-4
10 9 8 7 6 5

This book is for Jacy,
who will get there in her own sweet time

acknowledgments

Thanks to my two most intrepid and candid tasters, my brother Daniel and my friend Jon Mathews. Thanks also to Tracy Alexander and Bruce Ettinger for being such agreeable subjects. And thanks, as ever and always, to Michael Downing and Peter Bryant, who not only let me pay my rent in risotto, but would have me believe it's *they* who are getting the bargain.

This book is here largely because Margaret Garigan was at Harmony when I proposed it. Kathy Belden adopted it with enthusiasm, then nurtured it with insight and zeal. Thanks also to my agent Gail Hochman for, along with everything else, her genuine fondness for the food, and to her assistant, Marianne Merola, for being—mercifully—so reliable and resourceful.

Thanks also to the ebullient Ellen Rose of the Cook's Library for letting me harbor the delusion that my ideas are uniformly, incontestably brilliant. And thanks to Virginia Gilbert for staying on the line even when she knew I was about to read her another silly story from France, and to Liz Morehead for salvaging a troubled essay with an ingenious bit of editing. My travel agent, Karen Sullivan, compensated plenty for my shortsightedness, for which I'm grateful.

Finally, thanks to my parents, Iris and Anthony Shaw, in quantities too abundant to measure, for things too many to name.

contents

preface

I don't know why I decided, after all, to go to France.

I wasn't interested in the food (too fussy); or the people (too arrogant); or the culture (too ... *French*). I didn't speak the language. And there was the daunting legacy of all those good writers, food writers mostly, who've become known for the way they "know" France.

So, when I found myself with five weeks free, I can't say why I chose to spend most of them in a country I'd never been eager to see.

But I went that once, and my biases became untenable. It's hard to harbor a deep disdain for a country where the onion *tourtes* are so good, or for the people, who care that they're good—people who live as if living were the point of life, and who eat as if eating were essential to it all.

I went back to France four months later, traveling east, by train, into Tuscany, too, and discovering that while the French–Italian boundary is firmly fixed, the culinary border isn't as well defined. Then three months later, I went to Provence and Tuscany again, learning still more about the way people live and eat in a place where the two aren't quite as distinct as they've become here at home. I compiled this collection while traveling and hope that it will help you, too, discover new ways to savor whatever the seasons bring to hand.

introduction

The distinctive cuisine of Provence and Tuscany is the product of a fortuitous coincidence of geography and necessity. Geography accounts for the many ingredients regional dishes have in common. Necessity explains the rest.

For example, recipes calling for stale bread—as many from these places do—did not occur to epicures with other ingredients at their disposal.

Rather, they've come by way of the mother of invention, at work in a part of the world where to live to eat is no vice, where cooking has been a matter of contending with cycles of surplus and shortage; where, when disaster struck, ingenuity prevailed. Consider Florence, which has been spared nothing by man or nature. From time to time, civil wars and floods kept fresh food from getting through, and there'd be nothing to eat for months on end but flour, cornmeal, olive oil, and garlic. You might put a symbolic spin on the fact that those crafty Florentines, in their confinement, turned out polenta and *fettunta,* and see in this a grand triumph of civilization over the forces stacked against it.

Or you might simply be grateful that the Florentines were so resourceful. They more than made do, they made well—so well that today we eat by choice what they ate by default.

In France, the "fussy" food is up north. South of Lyons, it's what's fresh, what's fast, and what's affordable. For centuries the seasons have determined what goes on the table, surely a mixed blessing at times. A good year for asparagus, for example, could mean a good deal more asparagus than anyone would want to eat. To cope with a superabundance of one crop or another, cooks came up with many and varied ways to prepare it. Today, these variations no longer serve to tempt weary palates to yet another plate of the produce of the month, but to make the most and best of everything in every season.

VEGETABLE DISHES

For all of the fresh produce to be found in southern France and Tuscany, the region is no Eden for dedicated vegetarians. After all, relying on vegetables and grains at times was simply a concession to poverty; if the people of the region could have afforded meat, they would have eaten a lot more of it. As it is, bacon fat or beef marrow flavors many traditional sauces and "vegetable" soups, and bits of prosciutto turn up where you might least expect them. Lard frequently figures in the dough for pie crust and pizza, and many condiments, dressings, and salads contain anchovies.

The recipes in this book are meatless, so that dedicated vegetarians, as well as anyone looking to discover new vegetable dishes, can enjoy them. Even a small amount of meat or fish can affect the character of a dish, so to avoid compromising flavor, I've chosen recipes that don't call for meat to begin with, and a few that can be adapted with success. Spaghetti carbonara, for example, calls for bacon and eggs, but you can make a dish such as the pasta on page 137 that combines eggs and smoked cheese for a similar effect. *Bagna cauda,* a Niçoise sauce served with fresh raw vegetables, might seem a natural for this collection. But it's impossible to make it without anchovies.

Cooking in the style of southern France and Tuscany involves trusting your senses—including a sense of proportion, and common sense. There really aren't any authoritative "authentic" recipes for regional specialties, since no one could count on having the same quantity of any particular ingredient twice. In fact, it's fair to say that improvisation is more authentic than precision. (There, cookbooks tell what ingredients to use, but not how much; whether to bake or simmer, but not at what temperature or for how long. For example: "Sprinkle with olive oil, and put in a warm oven until done.") The recipes in this collection seem fairly literal but by nature allow a lot of leeway. The only imperative is terrific care in choosing your ingredients. Most of these recipes don't call for many ingredients, and the fewer a dish requires, the better each one must be.

Fortunately, it's become easier to find a good variety of fresh produce, much of it cut, washed, and ready to toss into salads, sautés, or stews. Fresh herbs, too, have caught on in a way that's heartening to those of us who used to have to haunt local greenhouses to get basil, chives, or chervil out of season. And you don't necessarily have to seek out a specialty shop to find imported cheeses, oils, and olives; many supermarket chains now carry a good selection.

Have these on hand or, next best thing, find a market nearby that can be counted on to keep them in stock.

Olive Oil: Olive oil is an *ingredient*. This isn't as self-evident as it may seem. Many cookbooks, with the best intentions, suggest that you try to prepare sauces, soups, etc., without it. The objective is to cut calories and fat, and the rationale is that olive oil doesn't contribute much else. But olive oil not only helps other ingredients release their flavors, it lends its own. Leaving it out will affect the outcome as surely (and as adversely) as omitting any other essential ingredient, such as garlic, basil, or tomato. Besides, most of these recipes call for so little (about 1 teaspoon, or 35 calories per serving) that it's hardly worth the sacrifice.

Regrettably, there's no substitute for the best olive oil. This is regrettable because there's a direct correlation between cost and quality. Good olive oil is expensive. Great olive oil, outrageously so. But having tasted how the best can transform mere salad into something sublime, I will scrimp on everything else so I can replenish my Manchiati.

I use two types of extra virgin olive oil: a less expensive and milder-tasting oil for cooking and a pricey full-bodied oil for drizzling over soups, salads, and vegetables.

Herbs: Fresh herbs, snipped and sealed in plastic packets, are now widely available at most supermarkets all year long, and I prefer them to dried for most of these dishes. Basil, oregano, rosemary, thyme, parsley, sage, and bay leaf figure most frequently in this collection. You can substitute dried herbs, but remember that drying removes the water and concentrates the flavor of the herbs so that you need only half as much (except for tarragon, which, unlike other herbs, loses flavor when dried; when substituting dried tarragon for fresh, double it).

Herbes de Provence: Several spice makers produce an assortment of dried herbs, which may contain basil, chervil, thyme, tarragon, sage, rosemary, marjoram, oregano, and parsley in varying proportions. Even when not specified, you can add a generous pinch of this to enhance the flavor of soups, sauces, and eggs.

Salt: Most of these recipes recommend seasoning with salt to taste. If you're worried about high blood pressure, leave it out. But I have to dispute those well-meaning cooks who claim you can get by as well without it; salt enhances the flavor of food, and many things simply don't taste as good without it. I prefer the taste of coarse salt, either sea salt or kosher.

Saffron: It's expensive, but if used sparingly, saffron is worth the price. Sometimes recipes suggest substituting turmeric, a less costly spice that gives food the same yellow hue, but which, I think, tastes like chalk. Consequently, I never use turmeric in place of saffron and don't recommend it.

Garlic: Look for firm heads, unblemished cloves. I prefer the kind with purple skin—it tends to be juicier than the pure white variety.

Tomatoes: Fresh is still best, if ripe and robust. Boxed, imported Italian tomatoes are best otherwise. If you must resort to canned, the unsalted variety gives you optimum control over seasoning.

Cheeses: Like olive oil, good cheese tends to be expensive cheese. But, again, it's worth it; 2 tablespoons of grated imported Parmesan has more flavor than a cupful of most domestic Parmesans. Besides, you'll need very little for most of these recipes, so they won't end up costing you much. The cheeses most commonly called for in this collection are Parmesan, Gruyère, *pecorino*, and *mozzarella di bufala*. Crème fraîche and *mascarpone* figure in a few as well.

CONVENIENCE FOODS

Most of these recipes are so easy, you only have to consider shortcuts for a few of them, such as crepes and tortes. Some convenience foods help you save time without sacrificing anything. But others defeat the purpose. This is my assessment of which is which.

Use
- Freshly prepared packaged crepes (those that I've tried are very good)
- Prepared "fresh" pasta, the kind sold in the refrigerator section
- Frozen prepared pie crusts, for quiche

- Imported Italian tomatoes, in boxes
- Canned vegetable broth, for use in soups, sauces, or risottos

Avoid
- Packaged peeled and minced garlic, which tends to taste tinny
- Vegetable oil when a recipe calls for olive oil or extra virgin olive oil (olive oil lends a particular flavor; substituting another kind of oil will affect the result)
- "Instant" polenta, which can be gummy and which tastes a little like plastic
- Bouillon cubes or powders for broths, which have a chemical taste that dominates anything added to them
- Frozen bread dough for calzone and pizza, which creates the wrong texture and upsets the balance between the crust and filling
- Canned tomato sauce, which may contain too much salt, as well as a strange-tasting combination of spices
- Grated domestic Parmesan cheese, sold in shakers or in plastic bags (less expensive than imported, but with, alas, virtually no flavor)

BASIC EQUIPMENT

These recipes are simple by nature, so you won't need an arsenal of sophisticated cookware. The basics are commonplace, inexpensive, and easy to come by.

Mortar and pestle: Why use a Stone Age implement rather than a food processor? This one gives you more control over the consistency of certain things, such as aioli, pesto, and rouille. When the objective is to incorporate ingredients into a concentrated dressing, a mortar and pestle is more effective than a food processor or blender, either of which may disperse the ingredients rather than bind them.

Mouli mill: Again, why puree sauces with a gadget you crank by hand rather than a push-button machine? To control the consistency. Food processors may puree too effectively, rendering a thin runny liquid when a full-bodied sauce is what you want.

Gratin dishes: Like cooks throughout southern France and well into Tuscany, I would be at a loss without these shallow, ovenproof dishes used to prepare *and* serve everything from gnocchi to crème brûlée. A 6-inch dish is for single servings, and a 14 × 9 × 2-inch will serve up to eight.

7-inch ovenproof skillet: A skillet that goes from stove top to oven is best for cooking crepes and baking small frittatas.

12-inch ovenproof skillet: A larger version is for sautéeing and for baking large frittatas.

Medium saucepan: This is the workhorse of Tuscan and Provençal cooking, for risotto, couscous, and pasta.

Deep saucepan or caldron: You'll need this for soups, pasta, and sauces.

Colander: Use to drain pasta and prepare vegetables, such as eggplant and zucchini, that must be salted and drained of bitter juices.

Cookie sheet: You'll use it for cooling and cutting polenta and gnocchi.

Kitchen shears: I use these for shredding and mincing fresh herbs. It's easier to snip herbs than to chop them.

Earthenware bowls: These bowls are handy for many purposes, including tossing pasta with sauce before serving, marinating vegetables, and giving dough a place to rise.

OPTIONAL EQUIPMENT

These items are helpful, but not essential.

Baking stone: If you're serious about pizza, calzone, or bread of any kind you will need a baking stone to regulate the heat in your oven and ensure a crisp crust.

Marble slab: The best surface for kneading dough is marble. You don't have to add much flour, so bread and pastry turn out lighter.

Food processor: Although I recommend a mortar and pestle for blending dressings, and a mouli mill for pureeing soups and sauces, the food processor is a help for chopping vegetables and kneading dough.

Pasta machine: Making fresh pasta can take all day without one. (In fact, now that there are several good brands of fresh pasta on the market, I never make my own.)

Microwave oven: Most of these recipes are so simple to prepare in a conventional way, that I don't give instructions for making them by microwave. But I use my microwave to steam vegetables for tossing into frittatas, *tourtes,* and whatnot.

If the French think you're under a certain age, they call you Mademoiselle. Otherwise, they call you Madame.

I don't have to tell you that to be called Mademoiselle when you're over that age is a jump start to the spirit, a great glittering gift to the ego. It makes you want to embrace all of France and vigorously declare your love for the place.

It's usually a truncated thrill. Shortly, someone with a colder heart (or keener eyesight) will call you Madame, and—thud—you'll be back to your senses.

But there was one time when I didn't mind being called Madame.

It was in Avignon, on a sultry evening, and I had my heart set on eating outdoors. The trouble was that others had the same hankering, and so every table at the place I'd chosen was taken or reserved. The hostess whisked me inside, where the air was stifling and still.

I was hungry enough to consider sticking it out. But the decision wasn't mine for long.

A voice, the reedlike voice of a cherub, began to sing an improbable lyric: *"Bonjour, Madame; bonjour, Madame."* The cherub, a child of about three, was standing on her chair and singing . . . to me.

"Bonjour, Madame. Bonjour, Madame."

The other patrons snickered, and the child's parents picked her up and turned her around. But this girl was irrepressible. She stood again, to serenade me some more,

"Bonjour, Madame. Bonjour, Madame."

The hostess had had enough. It seems there *was* a table outside, after all. She could seat me there now.

But I felt a wrenching at leaving this child. I'd been traveling for several weeks, anonymous and alone. What a comfort to be singled out, to be recognized in this strange and delightful way.

On the crowded deck, I ordered a Gruyère and herb omelet. I felt stunningly lonesome. I was lapsing into melancholy. But out flew my cherub. She found me, like radar. *"Bonjour, Madame. Bonjour, Madame."* Her voice carried above the rest, and everyone stopped to look and listen. She stood a foot away from me, singing those same two words, smiling into my eyes, which plainly, gratefully, smiled back.

Inevitably, her parents dashed onto the scene. They yanked her off and away tossing me a look to say, "We know it was a terrible intrusion."

And I murmured after them, "No. Not at all." My omelet arrived, bubbling and browned and flecked with fresh herbs, and I was, once more, at home in the world.

Sauces

The sauces of Tuscany and Provence were created by cooks who couldn't afford the luxury of mere condiments. Spare on ingredients and rich in flavor, sauces served to stretch whatever was in short supply and to enliven what was in abundance. And so they became essential to many dishes, rendering the dull delicious and the precious practical.

Aioli

Aioli is a dip with a kick. Serve it with an assortment of raw or lightly steamed vegetables, such as asparagus, artichokes, carrots, cauliflower, snow peas, string beans, or new potatoes. Or stir a spoonful into vegetable or tomato soup just before serving.

I get best results using a mortar and pestle, but it can be made with a food processor, too.

8–10 cloves garlic

1 raw egg yolk

1 hard-cooked egg yolk

1¼ cups extra virgin olive oil

Salt to taste

1 Using a mortar and pestle, grind the garlic cloves into a paste. If using a food processor, process the garlic into a paste.

2 With a mortar, grind in the raw egg yolk and the hard-cooked egg yolk until well blended. If using a food processor, add the egg yolks to the garlic paste and process until smooth.

3 Grind in the olive oil drop by drop if using a mortar so that it binds with the yolks. As the mixture thickens, add the rest of the oil in a slow, steady stream, stirring constantly. Or, with the processor running, pour in the oil in a slow, steady stream.

4 Season with salt.

Makes about 1¼ cups

NOTE: *If the mixture separates—if it looks more like oil than mayonnaise—it's easy to repair. In a clean mixing bowl, combine 1 egg yolk and 2 tablespoons of fresh lemon juice. Whisk in the aioli mixture, stirring constantly, until everything binds. Correct seasoning with salt to taste.*

La Rouille

There are so many "authentic" versions of this rust- (*rouille*) colored paste—one of several flavor-enhancing sauces for soups popular in Provence—it's hard to escape the conclusion that "authentic" is an altogether arbitrary designation. Serve rouille as a garnish for soup, along with toasted rounds of French bread rubbed, if you dare, with a slice of raw garlic.

½ cup soft bread crumbs

3 cloves garlic

1 teaspoon cayenne pepper

½ teaspoon powdered saffron

3 tablespoons olive oil

1 Soak the bread crumbs in water for 15 minutes. Squeeze out the excess water.

2 With a mortar and pestle, grind the garlic into a fine paste. Add the bread crumbs and grind again until well combined with the garlic.

3 Add the cayenne and saffron.

4 Gradually add the olive oil, stirring constantly, until you've made a smooth paste.

5 Transfer to a small serving bowl, and pass at the table to be stirred into soup.

Makes about ⅓ cup, enough for 6 servings of soup

La Rouille, Too

This one's more like mayonnaise, but it's also served with soup.

1 Grind the garlic in a mortar and pestle until you have a paste. Add the egg yolks and grind again until well combined.

2 Add the olive oil, drop by drop, stirring constantly, until it binds with the yolks.

3 Add the saffron and cayenne.

4 Salt to taste.

Makes about 1/3 cup, enough for 6 servings of soup

4 cloves garlic

2 raw egg yolks

1/4 cup extra virgin olive oil

1/2 teaspoon powdered saffron

Dash cayenne pepper

Salt to taste

Béchamel Sauce

1 Melt the butter in a saucepan over medium-low heat, and sprinkle in the flour.

2 Stir with a wooden spoon to make a paste. Continue cooking for about 3 minutes. Pour in milk in a slow, steady stream, stirring

2 tablespoons butter

2 tablespoons all-purpose flour

1 1/4 cups milk

Salt and freshly ground pepper to taste

Pinch ground nutmeg

constantly to eliminate lumps. Keep cooking and stirring until smooth, about 3 minutes. Season with salt, pepper, and nutmeg.

Makes about 1 cup

Crème Fraîche

It's my belief that the French have attained culinary distinction largely by adding crème fraîche to dishes that would be unremarkable without it.

Several of the recipes in this collection call for crème fraîche. You may be able to find some in the dairy case, alongside the sour cream. If not, it's easy enough to make at home.

1 In a glass or earthenware bowl, combine the heavy cream and buttermilk. Cover with plastic wrap and let sit at room temperature for 12 hours, until thickened.

2 Transfer to a glass or plastic container with a tight-fitting lid. Refrigerate for up to 5 days.

Makes about 1 cup

1 cup heavy cream, at room temperature

¼ cup buttermilk, at room temperature

Crème Pesto

This sublime combination of cream, cheese, and herbs answers that primal call, known to us all, for something supremely luscious and rich.

1 With a mortar and pestle or a food processor, combine the crème fraîche, garlic, cheese, and basil until thoroughly blended. Serve by the heaping spoonful on soup, pasta, or toast.

2 If you're not using it right away, store in the refrigerator, tightly wrapped, for up to 5 days.

Makes about 1 cup

½ cup crème fraîche (see recipe, page 25)

1 clove garlic, crushed

½ cup grated imported Parmesan cheese

½ cup minced fresh basil

Pistou / Pesto

A booster shot of basil for any soup—homemade or store-bought. Just swirl in a heaping spoonful of *pistou* before serving. It's superb, as well, on pasta, polenta (page 133), or Semolina Gnocchi (page 126).

3 cloves garlic

10 large basil leaves, minced

6 tablespoons grated imported Parmesan cheese

¼ cup extra virgin olive oil

1 With a mortar and pestle, grind the garlic into a paste.

2 Grind in the basil.

3 Grind in the grated Parmesan cheese.

4 Incorporate the olive oil drop by drop until everything binds in a paste.

Makes about ¼ cup, enough for 6 cups of soup

Sauce Tomate Crue

SIMPLE TOMATO SAUCE

One of the best ways to serve tomatoes in season—uncooked and dressed simply to accent their own true flavor. It's wonderful served plain, as a salad, or on top of angel hair pasta or lightly toasted bread that's been rubbed with garlic.

1 In an earthenware mixing bowl, combine the tomatoes, scallions, garlic, basil, and parsley.

2 Stir in the olive oil, and season with salt and pepper.

Makes about 3½ cups

4 pounds ripe tomatoes, peeled, seeded, well-drained, and chopped

2 scallions, white part only, finely minced

2 cloves garlic, crushed and finely minced

5 leaves basil, finely minced

10 sprigs parsley, crushed and finely minced

3 tablespoons extra virgin olive oil of the best quality

Salt and freshly ground black pepper to taste

A Mild Tomato Sauce

This is the sauce to use on Gnocchi di Patate (page 128), Spinach-Ricotta Dumplings (page 131), and Polenta with Walnuts (page 135). Try it also with the Plain Frittata (page 96) and the Garlic Bread Frittata (page 103).

1 Heat the olive oil in a large saucepan. Sauté the onion until soft and translucent, about 7 minutes.

2 Add the tomatoes and salt, and cook over medium-low heat until the sauce thickens, about 20 minutes.

3 Puree with a mouli mill or with a blender or food processor (be careful not to liquefy).

4 Return the puree to the heat, and continue cooking to the desired consistency. If it's too thick, thin with water or a bit of dry white wine.

5 Remove from the heat. Stir in the basil and pepper.

Makes about 3 1/2 cups

1/4 cup extra virgin olive oil

1 large onion, finely chopped

4 pounds ripe tomatoes, peeled, seeded, and chopped, or 4 cups canned or boxed imported Italian tomatoes, drained, seeded, and chopped

1 teaspoon salt

1/4 cup (about) dry white wine, optional

4 large basil leaves, shredded

Freshly ground black pepper to taste

A Piquant Tomato Sauce

This is the sauce to use on pasta dusted with the grated imported cheese of your choice. Try it as a pizza topping and a condiment for chilled frittatas.

1 Heat the olive oil in a large saucepan. Add the garlic, and sauté over low heat until the garlic turns light gold, taking care not to brown.

2 Turn off the heat, remove the garlic, and discard. Turn up the heat again, and add the tomatoes and salt. Cook over medium-low heat until the sauce thickens, about 20 minutes.

3 Puree the tomatoes with a mouli mill or with a blender or food processor (be careful not to liquefy).

4 Return the sauce to the heat, and continue cooking to the desired consistency. If it's too thick, thin with water or a bit of dry white wine.

5 Remove the sauce from the heat. Stir in the basil and pepper.

Makes about 3½ cups

¼ cup extra virgin olive oil

2 cloves garlic, thinly sliced

4 pounds ripe tomatoes, peeled, seeded, and chopped, or 4 cups canned or boxed imported Italian tomatoes, drained, seeded, and chopped

1 teaspoon salt

¼ cup (about) dry white wine, optional

4 large basil leaves, shredded

Freshly ground black pepper to taste

A Sweet Tomato Sauce with Cream

This sauce has such a lovely, subtle flavor, it's best for topping simple pastas, such as fresh tagliatelle or fettuccine. Or spoon some over risotto (page 117) or the Garlic Bread Frittata (page 103).

1 Melt the butter in a large skillet. Sauté the onion and bay leaf over medium-low heat until the onion is soft and translucent, about 12 minutes.

2 Add the tomatoes and sugar, and simmer until the tomatoes soften and lose most of their moisture, about 7 minutes.

3 Remove the bay leaf and pass the tomatoes through the mouli mill, or puree in a blender or food processor (be careful not to liquefy).

4 Stir in the crème fraîche and heat gently, stirring and taking care not to boil. Stir in the basil, and season with salt and fine white pepper.

Makes about 3½ cups

2 tablespoons unsalted butter

1 small white onion, thinly sliced

1 fresh bay leaf

4 pounds ripe tomatoes, peeled, seeded, and chopped, or 4 cups canned or boxed imported Italian tomatoes, drained, seeded, and chopped

1 teaspoon sugar

¼ cup crème fraîche (page 25)

5 leaves basil, minced

Salt and fine white pepper to taste

Crema ai Funghi

MUSHROOM CREAM SAUCE

This creamy sauce is great over pasta, polenta squares, or thick slices of lightly toasted French or Italian bread that've been rubbed with garlic.

1 Heat the olive oil in a medium skillet. Sauté the garlic and mushrooms to coat with oil, about 2 minutes.

2 In a small mixing bowl, combine the egg yolk and lemon juice. Stir in the sautéed mushrooms and garlic. Return the mixture to the skillet (without washing it), and heat over low temperature, taking care not to boil. Add the cream, season with salt and pepper, and stir until heated through.

3 Remove from the heat. Let cool slightly.

Makes about ½ cup, enough for 4 servings

1 tablespoon extra virgin olive oil

1 clove garlic, crushed

½ pound fresh porcini mushrooms, chopped

1 egg yolk

1 tablespoon fresh lemon juice

1 tablespoon heavy cream or crème fraîche (page 25)

Salt and freshly ground pepper to taste

Tapenade

Serve this salty spread on lightly buttered bread or toast.

1 With a mortar and pestle, combine the olives, garlic, capers, olive oil, and lemon juice to make a rough paste.

2 Add salt.

Makes about 1/3 cup

½ cup pitted Greek-style black olives, chopped

3 cloves garlic, minced

1 tablespoon drained capers

3 tablespoons extra virgin olive oil of the best quality

1 teaspoon fresh lemon juice

Salt to taste

Eating alone isn't the worst thing about eating alone. In fact, I like to have a chance, once in a while, to give myself over to a meal in a way that's not possible when someone is with me. No, the worst thing about eating alone is contending with condescending waiters, or those who treat you with contempt.

The younger waiter must've known this because he was trying like mad to make up for the other one, who'd shown me to a back table and left me not two seconds before returning for my order. I asked for more time, a daring thing to do, given his disposition.

When he cleared off, the younger one came on. His smile smacked of conspiracy— who knows what humiliation he had to endure when there weren't any single diners to pick on? First he brought me sparkling water, then a pink rose in a fluted vase. Then a basket of bread, and a pot of Provençal olive paste, the rich and luscious *tapenade*. And then he made way for the other, who'd come back for my order, not too happy to find on my table, which he'd so deliberately left spare, the water, the flower, and the *tapenade*.

Marking this, the young one winked. And for the time it took me to eat my meal—and I made sure it was a long time—we were in it together.

Soups

The first place turned me away. It was late, and the owner-chef was tired and ready to close up. So he sent me across the street, although, he said with a shrug, he wasn't sure Madame would feed me, either.

She almost didn't. It was late, after all. But then, as if to compensate for hesitating, she brought me soup. And what a soup. That tureen was testimony that Madame had not passed up a thing at the market that day: potatoes, beans, carrots, baby artichokes, tomatoes, onions, chard. She brought me bread, too, and croutons, and a little earthenware pot of red paste. Madame was quick; she caught me staring (blankly) at the paste and swung into action, ladling soup into my bowl, tossing a few croutons over that, then—plop—dropping a dollop of red stuff on top. *"Voilà,"* she said, handing me my spoon as if it were a summons.

I stirred the paste into the soup, which suddenly smelled of saffron. I had "discovered" rouille, and, so, the Provençal way of infusing soup with flavor.

The evening meal became known as supper on account of *soupe,* originally a dish made by placing a slice of bread in a bowl and pouring on top of it whatever remained in the pot used to prepare the midday meal. This also explains why soup is known, too, as *potage,* the contents of the pot.

Soup has all the banner traits of the foods of southern France and Tuscany: It's simple; it's soothing; it's thrifty; and it calls for nothing more precise than whatever you happen to have on hand.

A Basic Vegetable Broth

A full-bodied broth; the one to use in soups, stews, and risottos.

1 In a piece of cheesecloth, tie together the parsley, thyme, peppercorns, and bay leaf. Put into a large pot with the carrots, celery, onions, potatoes, garlic, and salt. Add water to cover by about an inch.

2 Bring to a boil, uncovered. Lower heat, cover, and simmer for 1½ hours.

3 Strain through a colander. Or, for a richer broth (to use for soups and sauces), remove the herb bundle and puree.

Makes 2 quarts

4 sprigs parsley

1 sprig thyme

8 whole black peppercorns

1 dried bay leaf

2 large carrots, peeled and sliced

2 stalks celery, sliced

2 medium white onions, thinly sliced

2 large white or red potatoes, quartered

1 large clove garlic

½ teaspoon salt

Water

Aïgo Boulido

GARLIC BROTH

Selon un vieux dicton, "L'aïgo boulido sauvo la vido"—there's an old saying, "Garlic broth will save your life." I don't know about *that,* but it's helped me keep a few colds at bay. Moreover, it's light and soothing, and very, very good.

1 Bring the water to a boil, along with the garlic, and simmer until the garlic is soft, about 20 minutes. Add the sage and keep simmering, about 20 minutes more.

2 Turn off the heat, spoon out the garlic, and transfer to a mortar. Mash the garlic and add the olive oil, grinding into a paste.

3 Stir the garlic paste back into the broth. Season with salt and pepper. Serve hot.

Makes about 2 cups

VARIATIONS: *For a richer soup, grind 2 tablespoons of grated imported Parmesan cheese into the mashed garlic, along with the olive oil in step 2. And/or grind a raw egg yolk into the garlic along with the olive oil. And/or at step 3, add 2 ounces angel hair pasta with the garlic paste, and cook until the pasta is done (about 3 minutes).*

2 cups water

6 cloves garlic

2 leaves sage, minced

2 teaspoons extra virgin olive oil of the best quality

Salt and freshly ground black pepper to taste

Soupe de Cresson

A SOUP OF WATERCRESS

This zesty soup gets its zing from watercress, a green so named because it's refreshing.

1 In a large saucepan, combine the water, potatoes, minced watercress, and onions. Bring to a boil and simmer over medium heat for 45 minutes until the potatoes are cooked through.

2 Puree the mixture with a mouli mill or with a blender or food processor (be careful not to liquefy). Return the puree to the stove and heat through without boiling.

3 Beat together the egg yolks and crème fraîche until smooth, and stir into the soup.

4 Adjust the seasoning with salt and pepper.

5 Just before serving, rub the bread slices with garlic to serve alongside the soup. Garnish with minced chervil and the whole watercress leaves.

Serves 6

6 cups lightly salted water

2 cups peeled and diced potatoes

2 bunches watercress, minced

2 large white onions, quartered

2 egg yolks

½ cup crème fraîche (page 25)

Salt and freshly ground black pepper to taste

Thin slices day-old French or Italian bread

1 clove garlic

Handful chervil, minced

Watercress leaves

Soupe de Haricot Blanc

A WHITE BEAN SOUP FROM PROVENCE

White beans abound in Tuscany, spilling over the border into the soup pots of Provence.

1 Rinse the beans with fresh water. In a large pot bring to boil 6 cups of lightly salted water. Add the beans. Stick the clove into the whole onion, and add it to the beans along with the quartered onion, garlic, rosemary, sage, and thyme. Let simmer for an hour, until the beans are soft, but not mushy.

2 Add the pumpkin or squash, and bring back to a boil. Simmer until the squash is cooked through, about 20 minutes. Stir in the chard, spinach, or lettuce, and cook for another 10 minutes. Turn off the heat. Fish out the garlic clove, and transfer to a small mixing bowl.

3 Mash the garlic and blend in the olive oil. Stir this back into the soup. Season with salt and pepper, and serve hot.

Serves 6

2 cups dry white beans, soaked 6 hours or overnight and drained

6 cups lightly salted water

1 whole clove

1 white onion, whole

1 white onion, quartered

1 clove garlic

2 tablespoons minced fresh rosemary, or 2 teaspoons dried rosemary, crumbled

2 tablespoons minced fresh sage, or 2 teaspoons dried sage, crumbled

2 tablespoons minced fresh thyme, or 2 teaspoons dried thyme, crumbled

2 cups diced pumpkin or any orange squash

20 leaves Swiss chard, stripped from the stem, spinach, or butter (Boston) lettuce, cut in strips

1 tablespoon extra virgin olive oil of the best quality

Salt and freshly ground black pepper to taste

Soupe de Provence

PROVENÇAL VEGETABLE SOUP

A spoonful of cream *pistou* in each serving makes this soup sensationally soothing. Serve with lots of crusty French bread—you'll want to sop up every bit!

1 Heat the olive oil in a large pot. Add the onions, garlic, leeks, and carrots, and sauté gently until the onions turn translucent, about 7 minutes.

2 Stir in the turnips, squash, potatoes, chard, tomatoes, beans, if desired, and parsley, sage, and basil.

3 Add water to cover, bring to a boil, cover, and simmer gently for 2 to 3 hours, stirring occasionally. Season with salt and pepper.

4 Ladle into serving bowls. Just before serving, swirl a generous dollop of Crème Pesto into each bowl. (Don't reheat after adding pesto.)

Serves 4–6

¼ cup extra virgin olive oil

5 large white onions, chopped

5 cloves garlic, crushed and minced

2 leeks, white part only, chopped

4 large carrots, peeled and chopped

2 turnips, peeled and chopped

1½ cups peeled and chopped squash (whatever's in season)

6 new potatoes, quartered

10 leaves Swiss chard, stripped from the stem and cut into pieces

One 16-ounce can tomatoes, with juice

1 cup cooked white beans or chick peas (optional)

⅓ cup minced fresh parsley

¼ cup minced fresh sage

¼ cup minced fresh basil

Salt and freshly ground black pepper to taste

Crème Pesto (page 26)

Soupe de Blette

A Soup of Swiss Chard

If chard has too much bite for you, you can substitute spinach for a milder soup.

1 In a large saucepan, bring the water to a boil. Toss in the rice.

2 In a piece of cheesecloth, tie the parsley, thyme, sage, and bay leaf. Add to the water. Stir in the onions and garlic, and simmer gently for 15 minutes.

3 Meanwhile, beat the egg whites lightly with a fork, and dip the chard leaves into them. Add the leaves to the soup and let simmer 10 minutes more. Turn off the heat, and remove the cheesecloth. Fish out the garlic and transfer to a small mixing bowl.

4 Mash the garlic and stir in the egg yolks, olive oil, Parmesan cheese, and nutmeg until well blended. When ready to serve, stir this mixture back into the soup and heat through, without boiling. Season with salt and pepper.

Serves 6

3 cups lightly salted water

⅓ cup raw medium-grain white rice

1 bunch fresh parsley

1 tablespoon minced fresh thyme

2 leaves sage, minced

1 fresh bay leaf

2 medium onions, quartered

2 cloves garlic

2 eggs, separated

30 (approximately) Swiss chard leaves, stripped from the stem

2 tablespoons extra virgin olive oil

¼ cup grated imported Parmesan cheese

Pinch ground nutmeg

Salt and freshly ground black pepper to taste

Soupe de Courge

A SOUP OF SQUASH

While we use nutmeg largely to season desserts, it's tossed into soups and entrées throughout Tuscany and Provence. Here it spikes an earthy, wholly heartening wintertime soup.

1 Place the squash or pumpkin, onions, garlic, bay leaf, and sage in a large saucepan. Add water to cover and bring to a boil. Let simmer until the squash or pumpkin is cooked through, about an hour.

2 Remove the bay leaf, and puree the squash mixture in a mouli mill or in a blender or food processor. Return the soup to the saucepan.

3 Add the cooked rice and add a bit of water, if needed, to adjust the consistency. Simmer, stirring for about 5 minutes. Season with nutmeg, salt, and pepper.

4 Serve warm, dusted with Parmesan or Gruyère cheese.

Serves 6

4 cups cubed acorn squash or pumpkin

4 large white onions, finely chopped

2 cloves garlic, crushed and minced

1 dried bay leaf

2 tablespoons minced fresh sage

1 cup cooked white or brown rice

Pinch ground nutmeg

Salt and freshly ground black pepper to taste

Grated imported Parmesan or Gruyère cheese

Soupe de Fenouil

FENNEL SOUP

If the wind's blowing right when you step off the train at Antibes, you'll be walloped by the aroma of garlic and saffron, the principal seasonings of bouillabaisse, a regional specialty. The same heavenly scented seasonings are at the essence of this full-bodied soup.

1 Heat the olive oil in a large saucepan. Sauté the onions and garlic until the onions turn soft and translucent, about 7 minutes.

2 Add the fennel and sauté until softened, about 10 minutes more.

3 Add the tomato puree, potatoes, and vegetable broth or water. With string, bind the bay leaf, thyme, parsley, and rosemary, and add along with the saffron and Pernod or other liqueur, if desired. Simmer slowly over low heat until the potatoes are cooked through, about 40 minutes. Check the liquid level from time to time, adding more water or broth if necessary. Remove the herbs, and season with salt and pepper.

4 To serve, rub a slice of day-old bread with garlic, then swirl it into the soup, along with a heaping spoonful of aioli or rouille.

Serves 4

2 tablespoons extra virgin olive oil

2 onions, minced

3 cloves garlic, crushed and minced

3 large bulbs fennel, coarsely chopped

1 cup tomato puree

2 cups peeled and diced potatoes

1 cup vegetable broth (page 36) or water

1 fresh bay leaf

2 sprigs thyme

4 sprigs parsley

1 sprig rosemary

½ teaspoon powdered saffron

1 tablespoon Pernod (optional)

Salt and freshly ground black pepper to taste

Thin slices day-old Italian or French bread, lightly toasted

1 garlic clove, halved

Aioli (page 22) or rouille (page 23)

Minestra di Patate

POTATO AND VEGETABLE SOUP

I prefer organic potatoes, which tend to be exceptionally creamy and sweet. But this soup is splendid with regular russets, too.

1 Heat the olive oil in a saucepan and sauté the onion, carrots, celery, and parsley until the onion is soft and translucent, about 7 minutes.

2 Add the tomatoes, and keep cooking until they start to break down into a puree, about 10 minutes.

3 Stir in the potatoes and water to cover. Simmer gently for about an hour.

4 Remove the mixture from the heat and puree with a mouli mill. (If you'd rather use a food processor, be careful not to overprocess, or it will be thin and runny.) If the puree is too thick, dilute with some hot water.

5 Return the puree to low heat and warm gently. Season with salt and pepper.

6 Serve sprinkled with grated Parmesan cheese.

Serves 6

2 tablespoons extra virgin olive oil

1 large white onion, chopped

3 carrots, peeled and chopped

1 stalk celery, chopped

1 bunch parsley, minced

4 pounds ripe tomatoes, peeled, seeded, and chopped, or 2½ cups canned or boxed imported Italian tomatoes drained, seeded, and chopped

3 cups peeled and sliced russet potatoes

Salt and freshly ground black pepper to taste

Grated imported Parmesan cheese

Ribollita

Tuscan Vegetable Soup

Don't worry if you're short one thing or another. There's no formula for this dish, which is named for the way in which it's prepared ("cooked a lot") rather than what goes into it.

1 Drain the beans and rinse with fresh water. Bring 3 cups of lightly salted water to a boil. Add the beans, red cabbage, and white cabbage. Boil until the beans are soft but not mushy, about 40 minutes. Drain the beans and cabbage.

2 Meanwhile, heat 2 tablespoons of olive oil and sauté the onion, celery, carrots, and parsley until soft, about 12 minutes.

3 Stir in the tomatoes, cooked beans, cabbage, potato, and fresh water to cover. Keep boiling, adding water as necessary to keep the mixture from drying out.

4 Cut the bread into thin slices and rub with garlic. Using half the bread, line the bottom of a deep earthenware bowl with 2 layers of slices.

5 Pour the vegetables and broth over the bread. Cover with another 2 layers of slices, and cover with vegetables and broth.

6 Season with salt and pepper. Drizzle with olive oil, and serve hot or at room temperature.

Serves 4–6

1 cup dry white beans, soaked 6 hours or overnight, and drained

3 cups lightly salted water

1 head red cabbage, sliced into strips

½ head white cabbage, sliced into strips

2 tablespoons plus about 2 teaspoons extra virgin olive oil

1 large white onion, chopped

2 stalks celery, chopped

2 large carrots, peeled and chopped

1 bunch parsley, minced

2 pounds ripe tomatoes, peeled, seeded, chopped, or 2 cups canned or boxed imported Italian tomatoes, drained, seeded, and chopped

1 large potato, peeled and diced

One 1-pound loaf stale bread

2 cloves garlic, halved

Salt and freshly ground black pepper to taste

Pappa con il Pomodoro

A TUSCAN TOMATO SOUP

When I was a kid, my friend Donna used to get to eat catsup with bread for dinner. It seemed like a privilege to me, because catsup was always my favorite part of anything I put it on. I didn't realize she ate it because she was too poor to eat anything else. Pappa con il Pomodoro (literally "Tomato Mush"), while served today in trendy trattorias, harks back to desperate times in Tuscany. And it may be this dish that Donna's mother, who came from Fiesole, was doing her best to duplicate.

This version isn't for paupers, particularly if you opt for imported Parmesan or *pecorino*.

1 Heat the olive oil in a deep skillet and sauté the garlic until it starts to brown. Remove and discard. Add the onion, celery, and carrot, and cook, stirring often, until soft, about 10 minutes.

2 Add the tomatoes, basil, and parsley and cook until the tomatoes break down into a sauce, about 20 minutes.

3 Add the bread, and about ¼ cup water to make a dense, mushy soup. Season with salt and pepper. Serve with grated Parmesan or *pecorino,* if you'd like.

Serves 4–6

2 tablespoons extra virgin olive oil

2 cloves garlic, crushed

1 white onion, chopped

1 stalk celery, chopped

1 carrot, peeled and chopped

4 pounds ripe tomatoes, peeled, seeded, chopped, or 4 cups canned or boxed imported Italian tomatoes, drained, seeded, and chopped

¼ cup shredded fresh basil

1 bunch parsley, minced

4 cups chunks of stale Italian or French bread

¼ cup water, roughly

Salt and freshly ground black pepper to taste

Grated imported Parmesan or pecorino cheese (optional)

Potage des Petits Pois

GREEN PEA SOUP

Catherine de' Medici, married off at age fourteen to the son of the king of France, and sorely homesick for Tuscany, imported several indigenous crops from the fields outside Florence so she could have, once again, a taste of her native land. The green pea was among them.

1 In a saucepan, heat the olive oil, and sauté the onions, carrots, and pea shells until the onions and carrots are very soft, about 15 minutes.

2 With string, bind together the parsley, thyme, bay leaf, and tarragon, and add to the pan along with the shelled peas. Add water to cover, and bring to a boil. Turn down the heat and let simmer over medium heat for 45 minutes. Season with the sugar and with salt and pepper.

3 Remove and discard the bouquet garni and the pea husks. Puree the soup with a mouli mill or with a blender or food processor (taking care not to liquefy). Return the puree to the saucepan. Adjust the consistency of the soup by adding more water, if desired.

4 Just before serving, add 2 teaspoons of olive oil.

Serves 6

2 tablespoons extra virgin olive oil

2 onions, chopped

2 carrots, peeled and chopped

3 cups shelled fresh green peas, half the shells reserved

3 sprigs parsley

1 sprig thyme

1 fresh bay leaf

1 branch tarragon

½ teaspoon sugar

Salt and freshly ground black pepper to taste

2 teaspoons extra virgin olive oil of the best quality

Soupe de Tomate à la Niçoise

A SOUP OF FRESH TOMATO

Tomato soup at its best, best of all when made with the red ripe tomatoes of late summer and early fall.

1 Heat the olive oil in a large saucepan and sauté the onions until soft and translucent, about 8 minutes.

2 Add the sugar, tomatoes, basil, thyme, clove, bay leaf, and salt and pepper. Simmer, stirring often, until the tomatoes break down into a sauce, about 20 minutes.

3 Remove the bay leaf and the clove, and puree the mixture in a mouli mill, blender, or food processor. If the puree is too thick, thin to the consistency you'd prefer with water.

4 Return the puree to the heat and simmer for another 5 minutes. Turn off the heat.

5 With a mortar and pestle, grind together the garlic and parsley. Add the 2 teaspoons of olive oil to make a paste. Stir the paste into the soup, and serve.

Serves 4

2 tablespoons extra virgin olive oil

4 large onions, thinly sliced

1 teaspoon sugar

6 pounds ripe tomatoes, peeled, seeded, drained, chopped

10 leaves basil

2 tablespoons minced fresh thyme

1 whole clove

1 bay leaf

Salt and freshly ground black pepper to taste

2 cloves garlic, crushed and minced

¼ cup fresh parsley, minced

2 teaspoons extra virgin olive oil of the best quality

Soupe des Lentilles à la Niçoise

SAVORY LENTIL SOUP FROM NICE

A small miracle, a lentil soup with fewer ingredients yet far more flavor than most others I've tried. This soup is even better on the second day.

1 In a large pot, combine the lentils, water, onions, and garlic. Tie in a piece of cheesecloth the rosemary, thyme, sage, oregano, and bay leaves or leaf, and add to the mixture. Bring to a boil, cover, and simmer over low heat for 1 hour 30 minutes.

2 Remove the cheesecloth bundle. Puree the mixture in a mouli mill or food processor, taking care not to let it become too thin. Return the puree to the saucepan and heat gently on low.

3 Tear chard into small pieces. Stir into the soup, cooking gently until the leaves turn bright green.

4 Stir in the olive oil, and season with salt and pepper. Serve immediately, or let cool, and refrigerate up to 3 days.

Serves 4–6

1 cup raw brown lentils, rinsed well

2 cups water

2 large white onions, chopped

2 cloves garlic, minced

2 large sprigs rosemary

2 sprigs thyme

2 sprigs sage

2 sprigs oregano

2 fresh bay leaves, or 1 dried bay leaf

1 bunch Swiss chard, leaves stripped from stems

1 tablespoon extra virgin olive oil of the best quality

Salt and freshly ground black pepper to taste

Minestra di Fagiolo

SIMPLE BEAN STEW

Rosemary mingles with garlic to send up a most promising aroma. And the promise pays off, in a scrumptious stew.

1 Rinse and boil the beans in the water for about 40 minutes, until cooked through.

2 Meanwhile, in another saucepan, heat the olive oil and sauté the garlic and rosemary.

3 When the beans are done, drain and add them to the garlic and rosemary. Add enough water to cover the beans by 2 inches, and stir in the tomato paste.

4 Bring to a boil, and add the pasta.

5 Remove from the heat. Let rest until tepid, and serve.

Serves 4–6

NOTE: *Resist the temptation to add grated Parmesan cheese to this dish; rosemary and Parmesan are a discordant combination.*

1 cup dry white beans, soaked 6 hours or overnight and drained

2 cups lightly salted water

2 tablespoons extra virgin olive oil

3 cloves garlic, crushed and minced

Handful rosemary, minced

1 tablespoon tomato paste

2 cups cooked short pasta (such as elbows, bow ties, or rigatoni)

Soupe de Fleur de Courge

A SOUP SEASONED WITH ZUCCHINI FLOWERS

A novelty from Nice. Provençal cooks commonly use zucchini petals to spice up soups and sauces.

1 Place the zucchini slices and potatoes in a large saucepan. Add the lightly salted water to cover, bring to a boil, and let simmer while proceeding with steps.

2 Meanwhile, heat the olive oil in a skillet, and sauté the onion, garlic, and basil until the onion is soft and translucent, about 8 minutes. Add the onion mixture to the zucchini and potatoes.

3 Stir in the tomatoes. With string, bind the bay leaf, thyme, and parsley, and add to the mixture. Continue cooking until the potatoes are cooked through, about 20 minutes more. Turn off the heat.

4 Remove the bouquet garni. Puree the soup with a mouli mill or with a blender or food processor.

5 Return the soup to medium heat, and bring back to a simmer. Season with salt and pepper. Stir in the minced zucchini flowers, and simmer for about 3 minutes more, so that the soup can absorb the flavor of the flowers. Serve warm, with grated Parmesan cheese to garnish.

Serves 6

2 cups sliced zucchini (1/3- inch thick rounds)

2 cups peeled and quartered potatoes

6 cups lightly salted water

Extra virgin olive oil of the best quality

1 onion, minced

1 clove garlic, crushed and minced

4 leaves basil, minced

2 pounds ripe tomatoes, peeled, seeded, and chopped

1 fresh bay leaf

2 sprigs thyme

4 sprigs parsley

Salt and freshly ground black pepper to taste

30 zucchini flowers, leaves only, minced

Grated imported Parmesan cheese

Minestri di Ceci

AROMATIC CHICK-PEA STEW

In thirteenth-century Sicily it was worth your life to be able to pronounce *cece,* Italian for "chick-pea." It was the word chosen by the "dialect detectives," and to flub was to be suspected of being—*gasp*—French, and so in cahoots with the unpopular usurper, Charles I.

I serve this dish all the time, and it's always pronounced "delicious."

1 Rinse the chick-peas in fresh water. Place them in a large pot and cover with 6 cups water. Add the garlic, rosemary, and tomatoes. Bring to a boil.

2 Cover and let simmer 1½ hours until chick-peas are soft.

3 With a slotted spoon, remove half the chick-peas, and puree with a mouli mill or food processor.

4 Toss the pasta into the pot with the rest of the chick-peas. Bring to a boil and cook until the pasta is done.

5 Stir the pureed chick-peas back in the pot.

6 Let sit, uncovered, for at least ½ hour.

7 Season with salt and pepper, and drizzle a bit of the extra virgin olive oil over the top. Toss and serve at room temperature.

Serves 4–6

2 cups dry chick-peas, soaked 6 hours or overnight and drained

6 cups lightly salted water

2 cloves garlic, crushed

Handful rosemary, minced

2 pounds ripe tomatoes, peeled, seeded, and chopped, or 2 cups canned or boxed imported Italian tomatoes

1 cup dry short pasta (such as elbows or bow ties)

Salt and freshly ground pepper to taste

Extra virgin olive oil of the best quality

vegetables

I love the French Riviera. Not for the swank hotels and sybaritic beach scene for which it's known. While there is a side to the Côte d'Azur that caters to high rollers and serious sunbathers, there's another side, too: affordable and down-to-earth.

The "sides" are both literal and figurative; most towns along the southern coast of France have two of them. There's that flashy beachfront. And there's the *vieille* (old) town, just a few blocks away, where villagers carry on a different kind of life altogether.

I discovered this dichotomy in Antibes, a slip of a city just east of Cannes, founded by the Greeks in the fifth century B.C. to fortify their principal port at Nice. Despite the imposing seventeenth-century fort at the entrance to the harbor, it's hard to imagine mobilizing a militia from Antibes, where the entrancing light and potent sun conspire to induce a kind of stupor. I can picture the troops, transfixed by the silver sky the morning after an autumn rain, stunned silly by the sight of the white-tipped Alps piercing the heavens to the east.

The old town in Antibes is for early risers. A boisterous procession starts at seven, resolute locals out to get the pick of the produce at the Cours Massina open-air market. But everything at the Marché au Antibes is so good that sorting the best from the rest is a petty enterprise. Apricots the size of apples and succulent as overripe plums. Mushrooms, some as big as your hand. Towering asparagus. Artichokes, eggplants, peppers—every display a master's still-life motif.

What do you do to such beautiful vegetables? As little as possible, the local cuisine would indicate. Steam and dip in aioli (garlic mayonnaise); drizzle with extra virgin olive oil of the best quality, dust with bread crumbs, and bake very briefly; marinate in herbs and dry white wine.

Panzanella

Ecco! (Here!) Yesterday's bread is today's tasty salad.

1 Dip the bread in water to moisten thoroughly. Squeeze out the excess moisture, and place the bread in a deep dish.

2 Top with the scallions, tomatoes, hard-boiled egg, and basil. Douse with olive oil, and sprinkle lightly with balsamic vinegar. Season with salt and pepper, and serve immediately.

Serves 4

2 cups bite-size chunks of stale Italian or French bread

2 scallions (white part only), chopped

2 ripe Roma tomatoes, chopped

1 egg, hard-boiled and chopped

5 leaves basil, shredded

Extra virgin olive oil of the best quality

Balsamic vinegar

Salt and freshly ground pepper to taste

Mesclun · MIXED GREENS

Mesclun means "mixture" and typically involves at least 3 kinds of salad greens, tossed with fresh herbs. It used to be a chore to clean and chop the greens. But now that packaged greens—cut, washed, and ready to go—are widely available, making mesclun is a cinch.

Some suggestions for greens (combine 3 or more of the following): arugula, escarole, red chicory, watercress, dandelion greens, lamb's-lettuce, chopped fennel. For the herbs, try parsley, basil, mint, chives, oregano, or summer savory.

Mesclun is meant to be a showcase for good greens, so dress it simply, with extra virgin olive oil of the best quality and red wine vinegar (3 parts olive oil to 1 part vinegar). For more flavor, whisk a teaspoon of Dijon mustard into the vinegar before blending with the olive oil.

Tossing is critical—turn the greens thoroughly but gently, so that each leaf is dressed, and none is drenched.

Tomate au Four

CHILLED TOMATOES WITH FRESH HERBS

An unusual salad that's exceptionally good.

1 Heat the oven to 375°. Pour half of the olive oil into a gratin dish. Cover with a layer of tomato slices. Sprinkle with salt and pepper, and strew lightly with minced thyme, parsley, and basil.

2 Heat the broiler. Place the red peppers, skin side up, on the broiling pan. Broil until the skin is well charred, about 7 minutes.

3 Transfer the peppers to a paper bag and let them steam for 10 minutes. Open the bag and let the steam escape. When the peppers are cool enough to handle, peel off the skin and slice into strips.

4 Top with strips of pepper. Cover with another layer of tomatoes, and repeat the entire process until you've used all of the tomatoes.

5 Drizzle the remaining olive oil on top, and sprinkle with capers and bread crumbs. Bake until the top is nicely browned and everything is soft underneath, about 20 minutes.

6 Let cool, then refrigerate. Serve well chilled.

Serves 4

3 tablespoons extra virgin olive oil

6 large firm tomatoes, cored and sliced into rounds about 1/3 inch thick

Salt and freshly ground black pepper to taste

2 tablespoons minced fresh thyme

2 tablespoons minced fresh parsley

2 tablespoons minced fresh basil

2 red peppers, halved lengthwise and seeded

1 tablespoon drained capers

1/2 cup fine bread crumbs

Caviar d'Aubergine

This eggplant dish is served throughout Provence, as a salad or as a spread for bread, toast, or blini.

1 Heat the broiler. Place the eggplant halves on a broiler pan, skin side up. Broil until the skin is buckled and charred, about 10 minutes.

2 Remove the eggplant from the heat and let it cool until you're able to handle it.

3 Separate the seeds from the pulp. Transfer the pulp to a large earthenware bowl. Discard the skin and seeds.

4 Stir in the garlic, tomatoes, olive oil, and lemon juice. Add the basil, chives, and parsley. Mix well.

5 Season with salt and pepper, and serve at room temperature.

Serves 4–6

VARIATION: *Substitute 2 tablespoons minced fresh dill and 2 teaspoons paprika for the basil and chives.*

2 large firm eggplants, halved lengthwise

1 large clove garlic, crushed and minced

2 ripe tomatoes, peeled, seeded, and chopped

2 tablespoons extra virgin olive oil

2 teaspoons fresh lemon juice

5 large leaves basil, minced

2 tablespoons minced fresh chives

2 tablespoons minced fresh parsley

Salt and freshly ground black pepper to taste

Salade de Chèvre

TOMATO AND GOAT CHEESE SALAD WITH BASIL

Chèvre in Provence can be painfully sharp—so I often used feta in this salad instead. For a zesty sandwich, layer the ingredients in a roll rather than a bowl.

1 Distribute the tomatoes evenly among 4–6 serving plates.

2 Sprinkle the garlic and the chèvre or feta evenly over the tomatoes.

3 Distribute the olives evenly on top.

4 Stir together the olive oil, lemon juice, mustard, basil, salt, and pepper. Pour evenly over each portion just before serving.

Serves 4–6

6 large ripe tomatoes, sliced

2 cloves garlic, minced

½ pound chèvre or feta cheese, crumbled

¼ cup Greek-style minced black olives

¼ cup extra virgin olive oil of the best quality

2 tablespoons fresh lemon juice

2 teaspoons Dijon mustard

2 tablespoons minced fresh basil

Salt and freshly ground black pepper to taste

Peperoni con Bufala

ROASTED BELL PEPPERS WITH CHEESE

An irresistible opener: Sweet bell peppers cradle soft mozzarella.

1 Heat the broiler. Place the bell peppers, skin side up, on a broiling pan. Broil until the skin is well charred, about 7 minutes.

2 Transfer the peppers to a paper bag, and let them steam for 10 minutes. Open the bag and let the steam escape. When the peppers are cool enough to handle, peel off the skin.

3 Transfer the peppers to a serving dish greased with some olive oil. Fill each cavity with *mozzarella di bufala*. If tomatoes are in season, tuck a slice of tomato underneath the cheese.

4 Mix together the olive oil and the vinegar. Pour over the peppers, season with salt and pepper, and serve at room temperature.

Serves 6–10

3 large red bell peppers, halved lengthwise and seeded

3 large yellow bell peppers, halved lengthwise and seeded

⅔ pound fresh mozzarella di bufala

2 large ripe tomatoes, thickly sliced (optional, in season only)

¼ cup extra virgin olive oil of the best quality

2 tablespoons Balsamic vinegar

Salt and freshly ground black pepper to taste

Poivron au Four
à la Niçoise

ROASTED BELL PEPPERS

One of the best (and simplest) appetizers I know. Choose firm, glossy peppers, and you can't go wrong.

1 Heat the broiler. Place the peppers, skin side up, on a broiler pan. Broil until skin is well charred, about 7 minutes.

2 Transfer the peppers to a paper bag and let them steam for 10 minutes. Open the bag and let the steam escape. When the peppers are cool enough to handle, peel off the skin. Slice the peppers into narrow strips.

3 Combine the garlic with the chives, parsley, and pepper strips. Toss with the olive oil, and season with salt and pepper.

Serves 6–8

6 large yellow or red bell peppers (or several of each), halved lengthwise and seeded

1 clove garlic, minced

2 tablespoons minced fresh chives

¼ cup minced fresh parsley

2 tablespoons extra virgin olive oil of the best quality

Salt and freshly ground black pepper to taste

Salade des Lentilles

LENTIL SALAD

I was equivocating, and Madame, watching from inside, wouldn't stand for it. She stepped out of the doorway and said, *"C'est le meilleur restaurant en Avignon!"* She said it with such conviction that I couldn't turn away. Whether it was, as she said, the best restaurant in town, I'll never know. But the warm lentil salad I had there was surely the best of its kind.

2½ (approximately) raw lentils

2 whole cloves

1 medium white onion, halved

1 large clove garlic

1 dried bay leaf

¼ cup high-quality red wine vinegar

2 tablespoons extra virgin olive oil

Salt and freshly ground black pepper to taste

1 Rinse and strain the lentils, then place in a saucepan. Stick one clove in each onion half and add to the lentils, along with the garlic and bay leaf. Add cold water to cover by 1 inch.

2 Cover the saucepan and bring the mixture to a boil over medium heat. Reduce the heat to a simmer, keeping the saucepan covered. Simmer until the lentils are tender, but not mushy, about 30 minutes. Check 2 or 3 times during cooking, adding ¼ cup more water each time, if necessary. By the end of the cooking time, all of the water should be absorbed.

3 Remove the pan from the heat. Discard the onion, garlic, and bay leaf.

4 Whisk together the vinegar and oil in a small bowl. Pour over the warm lentils and toss to coat. Season with salt and pepper, and toss again. Serve warm, at room temperature, or chilled.

Serves 6–8

Puree de Legume

VEGETABLE PUREE

Asparagus is a good example, but you can puree and season virtually any steamed or boiled vegetable to serve as a side dish or to use as a filling for omelets or a base for gratins.

1 Steam the asparagus until very soft, about 8 minutes.

2 Puree in a mouli mill or food processor. Transfer to an earthenware mixing bowl.

3 Stir in the lemon juice and season with salt and pepper.

Serves 4

VARIATION: *Heat the broiler. Transfer the puree to a 6-inch gratin dish. Top with 2 teaspoons butter, 2 tablespoons grated imported Parmesan cheese, and 2 tablespoons bread crumbs. Broil until brown and bubbly, about 2 minutes.*

1 pound asparagus, peeled and trimmed

Juice of 1 lemon

Salt and freshly ground black pepper to taste

Artichaut en Marinade

ARTICHOKES IN MARINADE

My local market keeps the baby artichokes in a little basket in the "precious merchandise" section of the produce department, so it was something to see great bundles of them, still on their stalks, heaped on the tables at the Mercato Centrale, an immense enclosed marketplace in the heart of Florence.

1 Remove the tough outer leaves from the artichokes. Boil the artichokes in a large pot of salted water for 7 minutes, until softened.

2 In a large saucepan, combine the water, wine, olive oil, lemon juice, and peppercorns.

3 Bring to a boil, and add the artichokes, celery, parsley, fennel, thyme, bay leaf, garlic, scallions, and salt and pepper.

4 Bring to a boil again, turn down the heat, and let cook, covered, over medium heat, about 40 minutes, until the marinade is reduced by half.

5 Strain the marinade into a bowl, cover, and refrigerate. Place the artichokes on a serving plate and chill.

6 When ready to serve, spoon the reserved marinade over the artichokes.

Serves 6

24 small (baby) artichokes

1 cup water

¾ cup dry white wine

¼ cup extra virgin olive oil

Juice of 2 lemons

2 teaspoons whole black peppercorns

1 stalk celery, leaves included, chopped

1 bunch parsley, minced

1 stalk fennel, leaves included, chopped

2 tablespoons minced fresh thyme

1 bay leaf

1 clove garlic, crushed and minced

12 scallions, white part only, chopped

Salt and freshly ground black pepper to taste

Asperges en Marinade

ASPARAGUS IN MARINADE

Asparagus season is so short, there's hardly enough time to whip up some hollandaise, much less try something new. But this tangy marinade is a perfect complement for tender young stalks and makes for a lively harbinger of spring.

1 In a saucepan place the wine, water, olive oil, lemon juice, peppercorns, thyme, garlic, scallions, and a generous pinch of salt. Cover, bring to a boil, and let cook 20 minutes.

2 Add the asparagus, stir, cover again, and turn heat down. Simmer gently about 20 minutes, until the asparagus is tender.

3 Chill and serve cold, as an hors d'oeuvre or salad.

Serves 6–8

1 cup dry white wine

½ cup water

6 tablespoons extra virgin olive oil

Juice of 2 lemons

1 tablespoon whole black peppercorns

1 tablespoon minced fresh thyme

2 cloves garlic, crushed

6 scallions, green part included, chopped

Pinch salt

2 pounds thin asparagus, stems trimmed

Brocoli en Marinade

BROCCOLI IN MARINADE

A zesty salad or side dish from Nice. Look for deep green broccoli, with full, firm heads.

1 Bring to a boil in a saucepan the wine, water, olive oil, lemon juice, a generous pinch of salt, peppercorns, parsley, thyme, garlic, and the scallions. Cover, and let simmer about 30 minutes.

2 Add the broccoli, and continue to simmer until cooked through, about 8 minutes.

3 Remove the broccoli from the saucepan and transfer to a serving dish. Refrigerate. Strain the marinade into a bowl. Cover and chill.

4 When ready to serve, pour the marinade over the broccoli, and serve chilled or at room temperature.

Serves 6–8

1 cup dry white wine

½ cup water

3 tablespoons extra virgin olive oil

Juice of 2 lemons

Pinch salt

2 teaspoons whole black peppercorns

1 bunch parsley

2 teaspoons dried thyme, crumbled

2 cloves garlic, crushed

6 scallions, green part included, chopped

3 large bunches broccoli (about 9 stalks), tough ends trimmed and stalks pared

Épinard au Four

BAKED SPINACH

Washing spinach can be an ordeal. I do it by putting the leaves in a large bowl of water, dunking them, and letting them soak for several minutes. The dirt settles to the bottom of the bowl. Then I remove the leaves, pat them dry with paper towels, and toss them into salads or something more substantial, such as this.

1 Heat ¼ cup of the olive oil and sauté the garlic until it starts to color, about 4 minutes. Remove the garlic from the oil, and discard.

2 Add the spinach and stir well to coat with oil; sauté about 2 minutes. Heat the oven to 425°.

3 In a mixing bowl beat the eggs well, then stir in the sautéed spinach. Transfer to a lightly oiled gratin dish, sprinkle with the remaining olive oil, and season with salt and pepper.

4 Bake at 425° until the eggs are set through but not dry, 10–15 minutes.

Serves 4–6

¼ cup plus 2 teaspoons extra virgin olive oil

2 cloves garlic, crushed and minced

4 pounds fresh spinach, chopped

6 eggs

Salt and freshly ground black pepper to taste

Haricots Verts
à la Provençale

GREEN BEANS WITH TOMATOES AND PINE NUTS

I'd already discovered that Middle Eastern food is pervasive in Provence, so I wasn't surprised when I ordered green beans in Aix and they came prepared the way my mother makes them. My mother is Armenian, and some of her clan came to America by way of Marseilles, which suggests that the beans I grew up with may have been French, picked up and passed on by Armenians. But the fact that the dish is made with pine nuts, common in Middle Eastern cookery, makes me think otherwise.

Use the long, skinny green beans for this.

1 Snap both ends off the beans, and strip away the strings.

2 Bring enough lightly salted water to cover the beans to a boil in a large saucepan, and toss in the beans. Cook until just crisp, 6–8 minutes.

3 Remove the beans from the water with a slotted spoon and place in a deep earthenware bowl.

4 In a mixing bowl, combine the scallions, olive oil, lemon juice, garlic, tomato, parsley, pine nuts, and salt and pepper. Pour over the beans and toss well. Let sit at least 10 minutes, tossing several times before serving, or refrigerate and serve chilled.

Serves 6

1 pound string beans

2 scallions, green part included, minced

¼ cup extra virgin olive oil of the best quality

2 tablespoons fresh lemon juice

1 clove garlic, crushed and minced

1 large ripe tomato, peeled, seeded, drained, and chopped

¼ cup chopped fresh parsley

2 tablespoons pine nuts

Salt and freshly ground black pepper to taste

Fenouil en Marinade

FENNEL IN MARINADE

I'm reluctant to say that fennel tastes like licorice, because that suggests something stronger than this sweet and subtle salad or side dish.

1 In a piece of cheesecloth, tie together the bay leaf, thyme, rosemary, and parsley.

2 Heat the olive oil, and sauté the garlic with the bouquet garni until the garlic begins to color, about 4 minutes.

3 Add the fennel, and sauté, stirring often, about 5 minutes.

4 Add enough water to cover the fennel; add wine, lemon juice, raisins, peppercorns, and salt. Let cook, covered, until the marinade is reduced by half, about 30 minutes.

5 Remove the fennel and transfer to a serving dish. Refrigerate. Drain the marinade into a bowl and chill.

6 When ready to serve, pour the marinade over the fennel and toss well. Serve at room temperature.

Serves 4

1 fresh bay leaf

2 sprigs thyme

1 sprig rosemary

4 sprigs parsley

¼ cup extra virgin olive oil

2 cloves garlic, crushed and minced

6 bulbs fennel, trimmed of everything but the bulbous heart, coarsely chopped

⅓ cup dry white wine

Juice of 2 lemons

¼ cup raisins

2 teaspoons whole black peppercorns

Pinch salt

Pois Chiches
en Marinade

CHILLED CHICK-PEAS IN MARINADE

Don't second-guess the French; lettuce may seem like a strange addition, but it serves to sweeten the mix.

1 Rinse the chick-peas with fresh water. Transfer to a large pot, with the water. Stick the clove in the onion and add to the pot, along with the lettuce. Bring to a boil and cook until the chick-peas are soft but not mushy, about an hour. Remove the chick-peas with a slotted spoon. Reserve the cooking water.

2 Heat the olive oil in a skillet. Sauté the garlic until it turns gold. Add the chick-peas, stirring often and taking care not to burn. Sauté until well coated with the oil, about 3 minutes.

3 Stir in the peppercorns, small onions, and thyme. Then add the wine, lemon juice, salt, and about ½ cup of the chick-pea cooking water.

4 Cover and simmer gently for about 40 minutes, checking occasionally. Add reserved cooking water, if necessary, to prevent burning.

5 Let cool. Serve chilled or at room temperature.

Serves 4–6

2 cups dry chick-peas, soaked overnight and drained

5 cups water

1 whole clove

1 large onion

3 small heads butter (Boston) lettuce, torn apart

3 tablespoons extra virgin olive oil

2 cloves garlic, crushed

2 teaspoons whole black peppercorns

6 small onions, peeled and left whole

2 sprigs thyme

½ cup dry white wine

Juice of 2 lemons

Salt to taste

Mange-tout en Marinade

SNOW PEAS IN MARINADE

The French have an apt name for the vegetable we, inexplicably, call the snow pea. They call it *mange* (eat) *tout* (everything). Our name may be more sonorous, but theirs is more informative.

1 In a saucepan, heat the olive oil. Sauté the garlic and scallions until the scallions soften, about 7 minutes.

2 In a piece of cheesecloth, tie the celery leaves, parsley, fennel, and thyme. Add to the saucepan along with the snow peas, lemon juice, wine, and water, salt, and peppercorns. Bring the mixture to a boil, cover, and cook briskly, until the marinade is reduced to about a third, about 10 minutes.

3 Transfer the snow peas to a serving dish, and refrigerate. Strain the marinade into a bowl. Cover, and chill.

4 When ready to serve, pour the marinade over the snow peas. Serve chilled or at room temperature.

Serves 4–6

2 tablespoons extra virgin olive oil

1 clove garlic, thinly sliced

6 scallions, green part included, chopped

6 leaves celery

6 sprigs parsley

2 leafy branches fennel

2 sprigs thyme

4 cups snow peas

Juice of 2 lemons

½ cup dry white wine

½ cup water

Salt

1 teaspoon whole black peppercorns

Fenouil Braisé
à la Niçoise

BRAISED FENNEL

Fennel is best when the bulb and stalks are firm, and its colors vibrant.

1 Bring to boil enough lightly salted water to cover the fennel. Blanch 5 minutes. Drain.

2 Heat the olive oil in a skillet. Cut the fennel hearts in half lengthwise and lay them, bulbous side up, over the olive oil. Cover, and let cook on very low heat about 15 minutes, checking often to make sure the fennel isn't sticking.

3 Add the tomatoes. Cover again, and let simmer another 20 minutes until everything is soft and well combined. Season with salt and pepper. Serve immediately, or at room temperature.

Serves 4

VARIATION: *You can enhance this dish in a number of ways: Add minced garlic to the olive oil at step 2 and/or at step 3 add a few tablespoons of dry white wine, a pinch of powdered saffron, or some snippets of minced fresh basil.*

6 bulbs fennel, trimmed of everything but the bulbous heart

2 tablespoons extra virgin olive oil

4 large ripe tomatoes, peeled, seeded, well drained, and chopped

Salt and freshly ground black pepper to taste

Aubergine à l'Oeuf

BAKED EGGPLANT WITH BÉCHAMEL

One of the more unusual eggplant dishes I've ever tried—and one of the best.

1 For the eggplant, bring to a boil a large pot of lightly salted water. Cut off the stems of the eggplants, and boil with the onion for 20 minutes, until the eggplants are very soft.

2 Remove the eggplants from the water and let cool. Halve lengthwise, and remove the pulp with a spoon, discarding seeds. Transfer the pulp to a bowl.

3 Prepare béchamel sauce and add the Parmesan to it.

4 Heat the oven to 425°.

5 In a bowl, beat together the eggplant pulp and the egg yolks. In a slow, steady stream, stir in the béchamel.

6 Transfer to a gratin dish and bake 15 minutes, until golden brown.

Serves 4–6

6 medium eggplants

1 onion, quartered

1 recipe béchamel sauce (page 24)

½ cup grated imported Parmesan cheese

4 egg yolks

Extra virgin olive oil

Aubergine aux Tomates

EGGPLANT WITH ONION AND TOMATOES

The trick to making this or any eggplant dish turn out well is choosing firm, slender eggplants with smooth, lustrous coats.

1 Peel the eggplants and cut in half lengthwise. Score each half several times. Sprinkle with coarse salt and place in a baking dish. Cover the eggplants with water.

2 Put a heavy plate on top of the eggplants and let rest at room temperature for 30 minutes.

3 Meanwhile, put the onions in a large sieve inside a large bowl. Sprinkle with coarse salt and stir well to distribute evenly. Leave 20 minutes.

4 Rinse the salt off the onions with lukewarm water and transfer the onions to a mixing bowl, with the tomatoes, and mix well.

5 Put 2 tablespoons of the olive oil in a baking dish large enough to hold the eggplants in a single layer. Heat the oven to 425°.

6 Drain the eggplants, rinsing in cold water. Pat dry with paper towels. Place in the prepared baking dish. Cover with the tomato and onion mixture.

7 Arrange the garlic cloves at even intervals across the top. Sprinkle with the remaining 2 tablespoons olive oil.

8 Pour the water into the baking dish.

3 large eggplants

Coarse salt

6 large onions, cut into rounds

6 medium ripe tomatoes, peeled, seeded, and chopped

¼ cup (4 tablespoons) extra virgin olive oil

6 cloves garlic

⅓ cup water

1 bunch parsley, chopped

9 Bake for about an hour, until the eggplants are tender.

10 Remove and let cool to room temperature before serving, sprinkled with parsley.

Serves 6

N O T E : *Salting is essential; it leeches the bitter juice from the eggplant and onion.*

Carota con Prezzemolo

PARSLIED BABY CARROTS

Good and garlicky; eye-catching, too.

1 Heat the olive oil in a large skillet. Add the garlic and sauté gently until the garlic is lightly browned. Remove the garlic and discard.

2 Add the carrots and stir until well coated with oil. Add enough water to keep the carrots from burning; cover and steam until the carrots are cooked through, about 10 minutes. Check often, adding water as necessary to prevent burning.

3 Turn off the heat. Season with salt and pepper, and toss with the parsley. Serve as a side dish, hot or at room temperature.

Serves 6

2 tablespoons extra virgin olive oil

1 clove garlic, crushed

1 pound baby carrots

Salt and freshly ground black pepper to taste

1/3 cup flat-leaf parsley sprigs

I Fagioli all'Uccelletto

WONDERFUL WHITE BEANS WITH SAGE

You can't escape white beans in Tuscany. But prepared as follows—stewed with tomatoes and sage—you wouldn't want to.

1 Bring the water to a boil, and cook the beans until soft but not mushy, about 50 minutes.

2 While the beans are cooking, sauté the garlic in olive oil until it starts to brown. Remove and discard the garlic. Add the tomatoes and the sage to the oil, and cook about 7 minutes, stirring occasionally, just until everything is nicely blended.

3 Drain the beans and add them to the tomato mixture. Season with salt and pepper. Serve immediately or at room temperature.

Serves 4

3 cups lightly salted water

1 cup dry white beans, soaked 6 hours or overnight, drained, and rinsed

4 cloves garlic, crushed

¼ cup extra virgin olive oil

2 pounds ripe tomatoes, peeled, seeded, drained, chopped, or 2 cups boxed or canned Italian tomatoes, drained and chopped

Handful fresh sage, minced

Salt and freshly ground black pepper to taste

Gratin de Chou-fleur

BAKED CAULIFLOWER WITH CHEESE

You can substitute tiny, tender Brussels sprouts or sliced green cabbage in this fast and tasty gratin.

1 Bring to a boil enough lightly salted water to cover the cauliflower. Blanch the cauliflower for 5 minutes.

2 Remove the cauliflower from the water and let it drain in a colander. Heat the broiler.

3 Transfer the cauliflower to a lightly greased gratin dish. Sprinkle with bread crumbs and Parmesan cheese. Drizzle with olive oil, and season with salt and freshly ground black pepper.

4 Broil until the bread crumbs and cheese have turned golden, about 2 minutes. Serve immediately.

Serves 4

1 large head cauliflower, cut into flowerets

¼ cup fine soft bread crumbs

¼ cup grated imported Parmesan cheese

2 teaspoons extra virgin olive oil

Salt and freshly ground black pepper to taste

Navets au Gratin

SIMPLY BAKED TURNIPS

Throughout the year, the French toss turnips into stews of all sorts. But they wait until spring, when turnips are most tender, to serve them as simply as this.

6 turnips

2 teaspoons (approximately) extra virgin olive oil

1 small white onion or 2 shallots, minced

1 clove garlic, minced

½ cup grated imported Parmesan cheese

Salt and freshly ground black pepper to taste

1 Heat the oven to 450°. Peel the turnips and cut each to about the size of a new potato.

2 Pour a thin film of olive oil into a 7-inch gratin dish. Sprinkle with the minced onion or shallots and the garlic. Arrange the turnips on top, and add just enough water to rest the turnips in.

3 Bake for 20 minutes, then test the turnips with the point of a knife. If they're still hard, add a little hot water and cook for another 10 minutes. Repeat until the turnips can be pierced easily.

4 Heat the broiler. Sprinkle Parmesan cheese over the turnips and broil until golden brown, about 2 minutes. Season with salt and pepper, and serve immediately.

Serves 4–6

Poireaux au Safran

A STEW OF LEEKS AND SAFFRON

Saffron powder is the closest thing to "magic dust." Add a pinch to a simple dish such as this, and—poof—it's simply sensational.

1 Heat the olive oil in a saucepan, and sauté garlic and scallions until soft, about 7 minutes.

2 Add the tomatoes and continue cooking until they start to break down into a sauce, about 5 minutes. Add the leeks, water to cover, and saffron.

3 Bring to a boil and stir in potatoes. Cover and simmer gently until the potatoes are cooked through, about 20 minutes. Season with salt and pepper. Serve immediately, at room temperature, or chilled.

Serves 4–6

2 tablespoons extra virgin olive oil

2 cloves garlic, crushed and minced

6 scallions, green part included, chopped

2 pounds ripe tomatoes, peeled, seeded, and chopped, or 2 cups canned or boxed imported Italian tomatoes

6 large firm leeks, white part only, coarsely chopped

Generous pinch powdered saffron

1½ pounds new potatoes, halved or quartered, depending on size

Salt and freshly ground black pepper to taste

Zucchini Rifatti

BROILED ZUCCHINI

Zucchini is bland, but Tuscans know what to do about that—pummel it with herbs and cheeses.

1 Place zucchini in a large colander or sieve, and sprinkle with the coarse salt, turning to distribute evenly. Set aside for 30 minutes, then wipe away the salt and moisture with a paper towel.

2 In a deep skillet, heat 1 tablespoon olive oil. Sauté the onion until soft and translucent, about 7 minutes.

3 Add the zucchini, tomatoes, and basil. Cover and cook gently until the zucchini is soft, about 7 minutes more.

4 Heat the broiler. Transfer the zucchini to a gratin dish and sprinkle with the grated Parmesan or Fontina cheese, the shredded mozzarella, bread crumbs, and 2 teaspoons olive oil. Broil until the top is golden. Serve right away.

Serves 4–6

8 firm zucchini, sliced into rounds 1/3-inch thick

Coarse salt

1 tablespoon extra virgin olive oil, plus 2 teaspoons

1 small onion, chopped

3 pounds ripe tomatoes, peeled, seeded, and chopped

4 leaves basil, minced

1/4 cup grated imported Parmesan or Fontina cheese

1/4 cup shredded mozzarella cheese

1/4 cup fine bread crumbs

Galette de Blette

SWISS CHARD GALETTE

Blette, blette, blette. In the *boulangerie: tourtes de blette;* in the café: *oeufs de blette;* in the bistro: *soupe de blette.* . . . It sounds sort of awful, and looks a lot like spinach—but *what* is *blette?*

    Finally, at the market in Antibes I saw the little handwritten sign and the large leafy greens behind it and recognized *blette* as Swiss chard. Not served much here, it's a staple in southern France, for reasons better sampled than explained.

1 Heat the olive oil on low, and sauté the shallots and garlic, stirring often, until the shallots are soft, about 6 minutes.

2 In a separate pan, heat the tablespoon of water, and cook the chard until bright green, about 3 minutes. Drain well, and add to the shallots. Also add the herbs, nutmeg, and pine nuts.

3 Stir well and cook about 5 minutes more, until well blended.

4 In a mixing bowl, stir together the eggs, crème fraîche, and *comte.*

5 Pour over the chard mixture and cook over medium heat until the bottom has turned golden, about 7 minutes.

6 Gently turn over with a spatula, and cook the other side. Season with salt and pepper, and serve hot.

Serves 4

2 tablespoons extra virgin olive oil

4 shallots, minced

1 clove garlic, minced

1 tablespoon water

1½ pounds Swiss chard, stripped from the stem and minced

2 tablespoons minced fresh parsley

2 tablespoons minced fresh chives

1 tablespoon dried herbes de Provence, or 1 teaspoon each minced dried basil, thyme, and rosemary

1 pinch ground nutmeg

¼ cup pine nuts

3 eggs, lightly beaten

¼ cup crème fraîche (page 25)

¼ cup comte cheese (a soft, mild cheese)

Salt and freshly ground black pepper to taste

Il Tortino con Zucchini

A TORTE OF ZUCCHINI AND RICE

1 Salt the zucchini, and toss it well to distribute the salt evenly. Set aside to drain for 30 minutes. Rinse the zucchini with fresh water, and dry thoroughly with paper towels.

2 Heat the olive oil and sauté the onion until soft and translucent, about 7 minutes. Add the zucchini, and continue sautéing until cooked through, about 5–8 minutes more.

3 Stir in the rice and half of the bread crumbs. Continue to sauté and stir until well blended. Heat the oven to 425°.

4 Remove from the stove, transfer to a mixing bowl, and stir in the eggs, Parmesan cheese, and oregano. Season with salt and pepper. Pour into an 8-inch tart pan. Distribute the butter and remaining bread crumbs evenly over the top.

5 Bake about 40 minutes, until firm and lightly browned. Serve immediately, or at room temperature.

Serves 4–6

Coarse salt

3 medium zucchini, chopped

2 tablespoons extra virgin olive oil

1 small white onion, chopped

2 cups cooked white or brown rice

1 cup bread crumbs

4 eggs, lightly beaten

½ cup grated imported Parmesan cheese

2 teaspoons dried oregano, crumbled

Salt and freshly ground black pepper to taste

1 tablespoon unsalted butter, cut into small pieces

Courgettes au Gratin

ZUCCHINI BAKED WITH CHEESE

By the end of August, "zucchini" can sound like a threat to home gardeners and everyone who knows one. Not so prepared like so.

1 Bring to a boil the lightly salted water. Add the garlic and simmer, covered, for about 20 minutes.

2 Add the zucchini, and keep simmering, until soft, about 15 minutes more.

3 Remove the garlic and zucchini. When cool enough to handle, peel the zucchini.

4 Using a mouli mill, puree the garlic and zucchini.

5 Spread the puree into a lightly oiled gratin dish. Sprinkle with chives and Parmesan, and season with salt and pepper.

6 Broil until the cheese is golden, about 2 minutes. Serve immediately.

Serves 4–6

4 cups lightly salted water

3 cloves garlic

6 small zucchini, ends trimmed

2 tablespoons fresh chives

½ cup grated imported Parmesan cheese

Salt and freshly ground black pepper to taste

Ratatouille à la Niçoise

A VEGETABLE STEW FROM NICE

Unfortunately, good ratatouille is not—as it appears—a simple matter of stewing a lot of vegetables together. Good ratatouille takes time, attention, and a slew of saucepans. There's nothing like it, though, when the zucchini is crisp, the eggplant just right, and the peppers as soft as they should be. I like it best on the second day.

1 Place eggplant in a wide colander, and sprinkle with coarse salt. Let it sit for 30 minutes. Dab off the moisture and the excess salt with paper towels.

2 Heat 2 tablespoons of the olive oil in a large frying pan. Add the eggplant and sauté gently until soft, about 8 minutes.

3 Heat 1½ tablespoons of the olive oil in another pan and sauté the zucchini until soft, about 8 minutes.

4 Heat 1½ tablespoons of the olive oil in another pan and sauté the bell peppers until soft, about 10 minutes.

5 Heat 1½ tablespoons of the olive oil in another pan, and sauté the onions until very soft, about 10 minutes.

6 In a heat resistant deep casserole, heat another 2 tablespoons of the olive oil. Add the garlic, and sauté until it starts to brown, then discard it. Add the tomatoes, thyme, parsley, and basil, and

1 medium eggplant, sliced into rounds ¼-inch thick

Coarse salt

8½ tablespoons extra virgin olive oil

2 medium zucchini, sliced into rounds ¼ inch thick

1 red bell pepper, cored, seeded, and cut into strips

1 yellow bell pepper, cored, seeded, and cut into strips

1 green bell pepper, cored, seeded, and cut into strips

2 large white onions, finely chopped

4 cloves garlic, crushed

2 pounds tomatoes, peeled, seeded, and chopped, or 2 pounds canned or boxed imported Italian tomatoes

5 leaves thyme, minced

1 bunch parsley, minced

20 leaves basil, minced

Salt and freshly ground black pepper to taste

cook over medium heat until the mixture is reduced to a thick sauce, about 10 minutes.

7 Stir in the prepared eggplant, zucchini, bell peppers, and onions. Season with salt and pepper. If the sauce is runny, place a lid over the casserole and drain the excess liquid.

8 Serve the ratatouille at room temperature. Or refrigerate and serve chilled.

Serves 4–6

N O T E : *If you're short on burners or frying pans, you can sauté the vegetables one at a time, transferring them to a separate bowl as each is done.*

During the famine that afflicted prerevolutionary France, agronomist Antoine Augustine Parmentier insisted that those French who complained of starvation were, in fact, suffering from stubbornness. Instead of marching on Versailles demanding lower grain prices, they should head back to their fields and plant potatoes. Parmentier said it was time the French broaden their diet and quit their dependence on bread in favor of other foods.

He had a good point—but not a great PR campaign. Among those promoting the spud was the most reviled person in France: Marie Antoinette. But the times were so desperate, and the potato so nourishing and delicious, it caught on despite the unsavory association. Needless to say, the potato fared far better at the hands of the French than did the queen. Potato dishes proliferated throughout the Revolution, including endless varieties prepared au gratin. Here is one that is easy and good.

Pommes de Terre
au Gratin

SLICED POTATOES BAKED WITH CHEESE

Use organic potatoes whenever you can find them. They tend to be creamier and more flavorful than the rest.

1 Heat the oven to 475°. Pour a thin film of olive oil into a 10-inch gratin dish. Heat on the stove top on medium, and cover with a layer of potatoes.

2 Remove from the heat, and sprinkle half of the Parmesan cheese over the potatoes. Distribute the onion evenly on top. Salt and pepper lightly.

3 Cover with another layer of potatoes, and pour the vegetable broth into the dish. Bake until the potatoes are cooked through, about 25 minutes. Remove from the oven.

4 Heat the broiler. Sprinkle the potatoes with the rest of the Parmesan cheese. Broil until the cheese turns golden, about 2 minutes. Serve right away.

Serves 4

2 tablespoons (approximately) extra virgin olive oil

2 pounds russet potatoes, peeled and thinly sliced

½ cup grated imported Parmesan cheese

1 small white onion, minced

Salt and freshly ground black pepper to taste

1 cup vegetable broth (page 36)

Le Patate en Ghiotta / Pommes de Terre aux Herbes

SLICED POTATOES BAKED WITH HERBS

Use organic russet potatoes whenever you can find them. They tend to be silky and more flavorful than the rest.

1 Heat the oven to 425°.

2 Put the olive oil and the sage or rosemary into a 7-inch gratin dish.

3 Place the potatoes in the dish, tossing to coat evenly with oil and herbs. Add salt.

4 Bake until the potato slices can be pierced easily with a fork, about 50 minutes.

Serves 4

1 tablespoon extra virgin olive oil

1½ tablespoons minced fresh sage or rosemary

2 large russet potatoes, peeled and sliced, about ⅓-inch thick

Coarse salt to taste

Patate in Stufa

A POTATO STEW

Rosemary and potatoes are a marvelous match.

1 Heat the olive oil and sauté the garlic and rosemary. When the garlic starts to brown, remove and discard.

2 Stir in the tomatoes, and continue to cook until they give up much of their juice, about 7 minutes. Add the potatoes and enough water just to cover.

3 Cover the pot and cook gently until the potatoes are soft, about 20 minutes. Season with salt and pepper.

Serves 4

1 tablespoon extra virgin olive oil

2 cloves garlic, crushed

¼ cup minced fresh rosemary

2 pounds ripe tomatoes, peeled, seeded, and chopped, or 2 cups canned or boxed imported Italian tomatoes, chopped

2 cups peeled, thickly sliced then quartered potatoes

Salt and freshly ground black pepper to taste

Les Champignons à l'Ail

MUSHROOMS IN HERB BUTTER

I would've said the girl was sullen, but, on closer look, I could see she was sodden. She'd had too much of the best of everything, and she was half past ready to go home. Preferably alone. But this was her honeymoon, so that was not to be. She was indifferent about ordering, which was a shame, since this was one of the better restaurants in Antibes. I hoped she'd stop moping once her food came. But she picked at her mushrooms, unenticed and unimpressed. She got a bit perkier on her second glass of champagne. Perkier, but no hungrier. Her groom ate, trying to coax her to do the same.

But she set her fork down on her plate and sat back while the waitress cleared it away. Her groom sat back, too. Slumped back. His plate was empty, and the table yawned between them.

I wanted to coax her, too, to shake her and tell her what I knew: that she'd leave nothing undone in the long life ahead of her that she would regret as much as those mushrooms.

12 large fresh porcini mushrooms, or fresh wood-tree mushrooms

2 tablespoons unsalted butter

3 cloves garlic, finely minced

¼ cup finely minced fresh parsley

1 Coarsely chop 6 of the mushrooms. Set the others aside.

2 In a saucepan, melt 1 tablespoon of the butter. Add the garlic and parsley and sauté for about 1 minute, just to coat with butter.

3 Add the chopped mushrooms, and continue to sauté until cooked through, about 3 minutes.

4 Remove from the heat. Place a heaping tablespoon of the sautéed mushrooms in the center of each of the reserved mushrooms. Fold each into an envelope and secure with a toothpick.

5 Without washing it, return the saucepan to the stove. Melt the second tablespoon of butter, and sauté the mushroom envelopes until well coated with butter and cooked, about 5–6 minutes.

6 Remove the toothpicks, and serve, fold side down.

Serves 4

Champignons à la Niçoise

MUSHROOMS WITH GARLIC AND HERBS

In Nice, this dish is made with cepes, a type of mushroom that's hard to find over here. White button mushrooms work as well, as long as they are very fresh and tender.

1 Separate the mushroom stems from caps, leaving both intact.

2 Bring the water to a boil. Add 1 tablespoon of the olive oil and the lemon juice.

3 Add the mushrooms and simmer for 2 minutes. Remove the mushrooms with a slotted spoon, and let them drain on paper towels.

4 Heat the remaining 2 tablespoons of olive oil. Sauté the mushroom caps lightly, until well coated with oil. Sprinkle with salt and pepper, and transfer to a gratin dish.

5 Heat the broiler. Chop the mushroom stems, and sauté them with the garlic, parsley, and chives in the same pan used for the caps, adding more olive oil, if necessary. Transfer to the gratin dish.

6 Broil to heat through, about 2 minutes. Serve immediately.

Serves 4

3 cups fresh whole white button mushrooms

1½ cups lightly salted water

3 tablespoons extra virgin olive oil

Juice of 1 lemon

Salt and freshly ground black pepper to taste

3 cloves garlic, crushed and minced

1 bunch parsley, minced

2 tablespoons minced fresh chives

Cavolo Nero

RED CABBAGE

Those frugal Tuscans come through again. This humble dish is delicious.

1 Bring a large pot of lightly salted water to a boil.

2 Slice the cabbage into strips, and toss into the water. Boil until tender, about 15 minutes.

3 Meanwhile, place the garlic under the broiler and broil until golden, about 2 minutes. Turn to broil the other side, about 30 seconds to 1 minute.

4 Rub the roasted garlic on the bread, and slice the bread into strips.

5 Dip the bread lightly in the cabbage cooking water, squeeze out the excess moisture, and distribute among 4 to 6 soup bowls.

6 Line a colander with paper towels. Transfer the cabbage to the colander and let it drain for several minutes.

7 Distribute the cabbage evenly among the soup bowls. Drizzle each serving with a bit of olive oil, and grind pepper over the top. Add salt.

Serves 4–6

1 medium head red cabbage

1 large clove garlic

4–6 thick slices day-old French or Italian bread

1 tablespoon (approximately) extra virgin olive oil of the best quality

Freshly ground black pepper and salt to taste

Gratin aux Carottes

CARROT GRATIN

Gruyère has a nice effect on this dish, which would certainly be too sweet without it.

1 Steam or boil the carrots until very soft. Drain thoroughly.

2 Heat the broiler. Puree the carrots in a mouli mill. Stir in the sugar.

3 Transfer the puree to a 6-inch gratin dish and top with the butter, bread crumbs, cheese, parsley, and salt and pepper.

4 Broil until bubbly, about 2 minutes. Serve right away.

Serves 4

1 pound carrots, peeled and thinly sliced

Pinch sugar

2 teaspoons unsalted butter

¼ cup fine bread crumbs

¼ cup grated imported Gruyère cheese

¼ cup finely minced fresh parsley

Salt and freshly ground black pepper to taste

eggs

If you ignored the dessert cart in the doorway (making a special effort to overlook the fruit charlotte, in Chantilly), the Salon de Thé seemed a safe refuge from rich bistro food. The menu offered poached eggs, for instance, on a bed of spinach. But the description was incomplete. There were eggs, all right, and spinach. But the spinach had been sautéed in butter and creamed with crème fraîche. And the eggs . . . ? I had to poke through a crust of Gruyère to find them.

What now? I'd come looking for something light and been handed a plate of lipids. But such lovely lipids. I polished it off, and ordered some of the charlotte.

In bistros and trattorias, I found poached eggs, baked eggs, and frittatas offered at midday and at dinner, too. While the soufflés and mousses prepared in other parts of France require precise measurements, timing, and some knowledge of technique, the egg dishes from Provence, and on into Tuscany, lend themselves to improvisation and whim.

Plain Frittata / Omelette Nature

When I was ten I saw Julia Child make an omelet on TV.

I decided I'd sooner try my hand at brain surgery. It seemed like a lot of trouble to go to, just to eat eggs. In Tuscany and Provence they seem to feel the same way. They simply pour everything into a pan and cook it until the bottom is set, then stick it in the oven until the top is done.

1 Heat the oven to 375°. Whisk the flour into the milk until smooth.

2 Beat in the eggs.

3 Heat the olive oil in a 7-inch ovenproof skillet. Tilt to coat the bottom and sides.

4 Pour in the egg mixture. Cook over medium heat until the bottom is set but the top of the frittata is still runny, about 6 minutes. Season with salt and pepper.

5 Put in the oven until the top of the frittata has set and turned golden brown, 3–4 minutes.

6 Loosen the bottom with a spatula, invert on a large plate, cut into wedges, and serve immediately.

Serves 2 or 3

1 tablespoon unbleached flour

½ cup milk

4 eggs, lightly beaten

1 tablespoon olive oil

Salt and freshly ground black pepper to taste

Frittata à la Niçoise

FRITTATA WITH TOMATOES AND OLIVES

1 Heat the oven to 375°. Heat the olive oil in a 7-inch ovenproof skillet. Tilt to coat the bottom and sides. Sauté the shallot until soft, about 5 minutes.

2 Add the tomatoes and cook until they have given up most of their juice, about 4 minutes. Stir in the parsley, chives, or basil and the olives or Tapenade.

3 Pour the eggs over the tomato mixture.

4 Cook over medium heat until the bottom is set, but the top of the frittata is still runny, about 6 minutes. Season with pepper.

5 Put the frittata in the oven until the top has set and turned golden brown, 3–4 minutes.

6 Loosen the bottom with a spatula, invert on a large plate, cut into wedges, and serve immediately; or let cool, refrigerate, and serve chilled.

Serves 2 or 3

2 tablespoons extra virgin olive oil

1 shallot, minced

2 ripe plum tomatoes, peeled, seeded, well drained, and chopped

¼ cup minced fresh parsley, chives, or basil or a combination

2 tablespoons chopped, pitted Greek-style black olives or Tapenade (page 32)

4 eggs, lightly beaten

Freshly ground black pepper to taste

Frittata di Carciofi /
Omelette aux Artichauts

ARTICHOKE FRITTATA

Fresh artichokes are irresistible. But they're so unwieldy, many etiquette authorities advise against serving whole artichokes to anyone but yourself and those intimates who don't mind making a mess in your presence. Here's a tasty, tidy alternative.

1 Bring lightly salted water to a boil in a medium saucepan, and add the lemon juice.

2 Meanwhile, cut off and discard the artichoke stem. Pull off and discard all of the thick outer leaves (this will amount to most of them), leaving only the fine pliable inner leaves. Cut the artichoke in half, then halve again. Using a paring knife, cut away the hairy "choke."

3 Boil the artichoke quarters until cooked through and tender, 20–30 minutes. Remove the artichoke from the water and let it drain on paper towels.

4 Heat the oven to 375°. On the stove, melt the butter in a 7-inch ovenproof skillet, and gently sauté the shallot and artichoke until the shallot has softened, about 6 minutes.

5 Pour the eggs over the artichoke. Season with salt and pepper.

6 Cook over medium heat until the bottom is set but the top is still runny, about 5 minutes. Sprinkle with the chives.

2 tablespoons fresh lemon juice

1 whole artichoke

2 tablespoons unsalted butter

1 shallot, minced

4 eggs, lightly beaten

1 tablespoon minced fresh chives

Salt and freshly ground black pepper to taste

7 Place the skillet in the oven until the top of the frittata has set and browned, 3–4 minutes.

8 Loosen the bottom of the frittata with a spatula, invert it on a large plate, cut into wedges, and serve immediately. Or let it cool, then chill, and serve cold.

Serves 2

N O T E : *When fresh whole artichokes aren't available, substitute 1 cup frozen artichoke hearts, thawed, thoroughly drained, and thinly sliced.*

Frittata di Asparagi / Omelette aux Asperges

ASPARAGUS FRITTATA

I was so desperate for a taste of spring, I ordered this dish two days in a row when the season's first asparagus arrived in Antibes.

1 Tie the asparagus into a bunch. Bring about 3 inches of lightly salted water to a boil in a deep pot. Stand the asparagus up in the pot, cover, and steam until bright green, about 10 minutes.

2 Remove from the water, and drain on paper towels. Cut into pieces about an inch long.

3 Heat the oven to 375°. Melt the butter in a 7-inch ovenproof skillet, and gently sauté the asparagus with the shallot until the shallot is softened, about 6 minutes.

4 Pour the eggs over the asparagus.

5 Cook over medium heat until the bottom is set, but the top of the frittata is still runny, about 5 minutes. Sprinkle with grated Parmesan cheese, and season with salt and pepper.

6 Place the skillet in the oven until the top of the frittata has set and browned, 3–4 minutes.

7 Loosen the bottom with a spatula, invert on a large plate, cut into wedges, and serve; or let it cool, then chill, and serve cold.

Serves 2

8–10 stalks asparagus, peeled and trimmed to consistent length

2 tablespoons unsalted butter

1 shallot, thinly sliced

4 eggs, lightly beaten

2 tablespoons grated imported Parmesan cheese

Salt and freshly ground black pepper to taste

La Frittata di Pasta

PASTA FRITTATA

Only the Tuscans could make a delicacy of leftover pasta. *E eccola*—"and this is it."

1 Heat the oven to 375°. Heat the olive oil in an ovenproof 7-inch skillet, swirling to coat the bottom and sides.

2 In a mixing bowl stir together the eggs and the leftover pasta.

3 Pour the egg and pasta mixture into the prepared skillet and cook over medium heat until the bottom is set but the top of the frittata is still runny, about 5 minutes.

4 Place the skillet in the oven until the top of the frittata has set and browned, 3–4 minutes.

5 Loosen the bottom of the frittata with a spatula, invert on a large plate, cut into wedges, and serve immediately; or let cool, then chill, and serve cold.

Serves 2

1 tablespoon extra virgin olive oil

4 eggs, lightly beaten

⅔ cup leftover pasta in sauce of any kind

La Frittata con Patate / Omelette aux Pommes de Terre

2 teaspoons extra virgin olive oil

1 tablespoon unsalted butter

1 russet potato, peeled and sliced into very thin rounds

Coarse salt and freshly ground pepper to taste

4 eggs, lightly beaten

POTATO FRITTATA

1 Heat the oven to 375°. Heat the oil and butter together, to coat the bottom and sides of a 7-inch ovenproof skillet.

2 Add the potato slices in a single layer. Cook gently, turning to cook both sides, about 20 minutes. Season with salt and pepper.

3 Pour the eggs over the potatoes.

4 Cook over medium heat until the bottom is set, but the top of the frittata is still runny, about 5 minutes.

5 Place the skillet in the oven until the top of the frittata has set and browned, 3–4 minutes.

6 Loosen the bottom of the frittata with a spatula, invert on a large plate, cut into wedges, and serve immediately; or let cool, then chill, and serve cold.

Serves 2

VARIATION: *Proceed through step 2. Then whisk ¼ cup crème fraîche (page 25) into the eggs. Continue to step 4. At step 4, once the bottom has set, sprinkle with ¼ cup grated Gruyère cheese. Then continue according to the directions.*

Frittata di Pane

GARLIC BREAD FRITTATA

An unlikely combination, perhaps, but a good one, without doubt!

1 Heat the oven to 375°. Heat the olive oil in an ovenproof 7-inch skillet, swirling to coat the bottom and sides.

2 Rub the bread with the garlic and sauté the bread in the olive oil until lightly coated.

3 Beat together the eggs and milk, add salt and pepper, and pour over the bread.

4 Cook over medium heat until the bottom is set, but the top of the frittata is still runny, about 5 minutes.

5 Place the skillet in the oven until the top has set and browned, 3–4 minutes.

6 Loosen the bottom of the frittata with a spatula, invert on a large plate, cut into wedges, and serve right away; or let chill and serve cold.

Serves 2

2 tablespoons extra virgin olive oil

4 thin slices stale Italian or French bread

1 clove garlic, sliced in half

4 eggs, lightly beaten

½ cup milk

Salt and freshly ground black pepper to taste

I'm sure anthropologists, historians, and sociologists have some interesting things to say about the antipathy between the French and the Italians. The fact is, they really dislike each other. As I found—not for the first time, nor for the last—one night in Florence.

The waiters (Italian) were flirting with me, stirring the indignation of the men (French) at the next table, whose mission became to rescue me, not just from the present "danger" but from the country itself. They offered to drive me, to France, the next day.

I wasn't planning to leave until the day after that, but, what the heck. Getting there on my own meant changing trains at Milan's maddening main station (a place with only one advantage over the Bermuda triangle: the food's better), which in turn meant tacking an extra day onto my trip, while taking a year, or ten, off my life. These men, George and Michel—shipping executives from Nice—seemed harmless enough, so I said sure.

They picked me up at my hotel, and we took off. Everything in Italy to them was contemptible. The streetlights ("Too dim!"); the street signs ("Unreadable!"); the people ("Crooks!"). Michel leaned over the wheel, hell-bent for the border. But, just short of the *autostrada*, he swerved suddenly. I cringed, sure he'd lost control of the car.

But no, he'd lost control of himself, undone by a hand-lettered sign posted by the curb: FUNGHI. We pulled into the lot, and Michel bolted for the stand. George followed, promising to return shortly.

It seems their disdain for things Italian didn't extend to mushrooms. Fifteen minutes later, they were back, stacking flats of porcini into the trunk.

La Frittata con i Funghi

PORCINI MUSHROOM FRITTATA

Porcini are rich tasting and hearty, the meatiest of mushrooms.

1 Slice the mushrooms into strips. Heat the oven to 375°.

2 Heat the oil in a 7-inch ovenproof skillet, and gently sauté the garlic until it just starts to turn golden, about 5 minutes. Add the mushrooms and parsley, and sauté to coat well with the oil and garlic.

3 Pour the eggs over the mushrooms.

4 Cook over medium heat until the bottom is set, but the top is still runny, about 5 minutes.

5 Place the skillet in the oven until the top of the frittata has set and browned, 3–4 minutes.

6 Loosen the bottom of the frittata with a spatula, invert on a large plate, cut into wedges, and serve immediately; or let cool, then chill, and serve cold.

7 Sprinkle with salt and pepper.

Serves 2

2 large caps fresh porcini mushrooms, or 2 whole fresh oyster or wood-tree mushrooms

2 tablespoons extra virgin olive oil

2 cloves garlic, finely minced

3 tablespoons minced fresh parsley

4 eggs, lightly beaten

Salt and freshly ground black pepper to taste

Trouchia à la Niçoise

A *trouchia* is really a big, baked omelet. Sturdy, substantial, and tasty hot or cold, it's perfect for picnics.

1 In a large mixing bowl, stir together the eggs, chard or spinach, chervil, parsley, basil, and cheese. Season with salt and pepper.

2 Grease a deep 12-inch skillet. Warm over medium heat, and pour in the eggs, spreading to even them out. Turn down the heat, and cover the skillet with a heat-resistant plate of the same circumference.

3 Cook the *trouchia* slowly over low heat, checking every 3 minutes or so, until it's almost set but the top is still runny. This should take 8–10 minutes. Using a pot holder to protect your hands, lift off the plate, and set it down within reach.

4 Loosen the bottom of the *trouchia* with a spatula, and slide it, runny side up, onto the plate. Grease the pan again and return to medium heat. Swiftly flip the *trouchia* into the pan to cook the other side.

5 Lower the heat, cover the pan with the plate again, and cook until thoroughly set, 4–6 minutes more.

Serves 5 or 6

8 eggs, lightly beaten

2 large bunches Swiss chard or fresh spinach, leaves stripped from the stems and finely chopped

1 bunch chervil, minced

1 bunch parsley, minced

10 leaves basil, minced

½ cup grated imported Parmesan cheese

Salt and freshly ground black pepper to taste

Tian au Riz

SEASONAL VEGETABLES BAKED WITH EGGS, RICE, AND CHEESE

In Nice, everything gets tossed into *tian*: red squash in winter, zucchini in summer, artichokes and asparagus in spring. Regardless of the season, the basics remain: chard, onion, parsley or basil, eggs, rice, Parmesan cheese, and olive oil.

1 Bring to a boil enough lightly salted water to cover the zucchini. Blanch the zucchini until a knife pierces it easily, about 5 minutes. Remove with a slotted spoon and drain thoroughly. Puree with a mouli mill or a food processor.

2 Steam the chard in very little water until cooked, about 2 minutes.

3 Heat the olive oil in a deep skillet and sauté the onions and garlic until the onions are soft and translucent, about 7 minutes. Add the pureed zucchini, the chard, and the rice, and stir to blend. Heat the oven to 425°. Lightly grease a 10-inch gratin pan.

4 Transfer the zucchini mixture to a large mixing bowl. Beat in the eggs, basil, parsley, Parmesan cheese, and salt and pepper. Spread the mixture into the prepared gratin dish. Bake until set, about 30 minutes.

5 Let cool to room temperature before serving.

Serves 4–6

4 cups chopped zucchini

1 bunch Swiss chard, leaves stripped from stems and chopped

2 tablespoons extra virgin olive oil

2 onions, chopped

1 clove garlic, crushed and minced

2 cups cooked medium-grain white rice

3 eggs, lightly beaten

¼ cup minced fresh basil

1 bunch parsley, minced

1 cup grated imported Parmesan cheese

Salt and freshly ground black pepper to taste

Oeufs et Épinard

POACHED EGGS WITH CREAMED SPINACH

So much for the idea that poached eggs make for a spartan re-
past. . . .

1 Heat the oven to 350°.

2 Lightly butter an individual gratin dish. Spread the cooked
spinach evenly across the bottom of the gratin dish and heat it
gently on the stove on low.

3 Top the spinach with the poached eggs, cover with crème
fraîche or cream, and sprinkle with the cheese.

4 Bake until the cheese melts, about 2 minutes. Serve hot.

Serves 2

*1 pound fresh spinach,
cooked, squeezed dry,
and chopped*

2 eggs, poached

*2 tablespoons crème
fraîche (page 25) or heavy
cream*

*2 tablespoons grated
Gruyère cheese*

Uova al Forno

BAKED EGGS FLORENTINE

Yet another wonderful way to enjoy spinach and eggs.

1 Prepare the béchamel sauce.

2 If using fresh spinach, place it in a small saucepan. Cover and let sit over low heat until bright green, about 2 minutes. Remove the spinach from the heat, and squeeze out excess moisture. Skip this step if you're using frozen spinach.

3 Heat the oven to 400°. In a mixing bowl, combine the spinach and the butter. Stir in half of the béchamel. Transfer the spinach mixture to a gratin dish, and make 4 evenly spaced indentations.

4 Crack an egg over each indentation. Pour the remaining béchamel sauce over the eggs, and sprinkle the Parmesan cheese on top.

5 Bake until the whites of the eggs have set, about 8–10 minutes. Serve right away.

Serves 4

1 recipe béchamel sauce (page 24)

2 pounds fresh spinach, chopped, or 2 pounds frozen chopped spinach, thawed and well drained

2 tablespoons unsalted butter, softened

4 eggs

¼ cup grated imported Parmesan cheese

Whenever things got a little too routine while I was in France, I'd pack a lunch and hop a train. Any train. Sometimes I'd let two hours go by before I'd ask where it was going. And one time I just got off at Arles.

I walked to the Rhône and ate the bread I'd brought from Antibes, the sweet chunk of Pyrenees Muenster, and the basket of berries, meanwhile playing a game that came back to me from childhood, wondering if Julius Caesar or Vincent van Gogh or Henry James had sat on *this spot* or touched *this stone*. Possibly. Each had spent time in Arles. Caesar built an arena there, a huge stadium, that gapes as if to swallow the sun that is so strong in that part of France. Van Gogh painted there—his house, his café, his craggy pathway home. And Henry James wrote there—lovingly and ironically, about the "other" France, the France that is not Paris.

All that contemplation made me thirsty, so I followed the sign for cold drinks. The sign told less than half the story; there was hot, simple food there, too, including a most appetizing mess of tomatoes, onions, and peppers—like a *piperade,* but with fried eggs on top instead of scrambled eggs throughout. Shoe box, side street—the place was a find. Too bad I hadn't found it sooner. I bought my Badoit and backed out, resenting my lunch.

Luck and trains often conspire, but rarely in favorable ways. This time was different. At the station they said the train to Antibes would arrive four hours late. The other passengers on the platform groaned. But I went back and had that *piperade.*

Piperade Arlésien

EGGS AND PEPPERS

1 In a deep heavy skillet, heat the olive oil and sauté the onions slowly until soft and golden, about 40 minutes.

2 Add the red and green peppers and continue cooking until soft, about 20 minutes more.

3 Stir in the tomatoes. Season with marjoram or chives and salt and pepper. Continue cooking until reduced to a dense stew, about 20 minutes more.

4 Transfer to a deep serving dish, and arrange the eggs on top. Serve immediately.

Serves 4

3 tablespoons extra virgin olive oil

4 onions, thinly sliced

2 red bell peppers, cored, seeded, and sliced lengthwise into strips

2 green bell peppers, cored, seeded, and sliced lengthwise into strips

2 pounds ripe tomatoes, peeled, seeded, and drained, or 2 pounds canned or boxed imported Italian tomatoes, drained and chopped

Pinch dried marjoram, crumbled, or 1 tablespoon minced fresh chives

Salt and freshly ground black pepper to taste

4 eggs, poached or fried

Aromi con Uova

POACHED EGGS WITH HERBS

A split-second supper. Especially satisfying with soup.

1 Place a slice of mozzarella on each piece of toast. Top each with a poached or fried egg.

2 Sprinkle ¼ of each of the minced fresh herbs on each egg. Season with salt and pepper.

3 Drizzle ¼ teaspoon of the olive oil on each portion. Serve immediately.

Serves 4

4 slices (about 4 ounces) fresh mozzarella di bufala

4 thick slices Italian or French bread, lightly toasted

4 eggs, poached or fried

1 tablespoon each minced fresh basil, parsley, and oregano

Salt and freshly ground black pepper to taste

1 teaspoon extra virgin olive oil of the best quality

Oeufs à la Provençale

POACHED EGGS WITH HERBS, TOMATOES, AND CHEESE

Here's another swift and simple supper, from the wine bars and tea salons of southern France.

1 Heat the oven to 475°. Put the butter or oil into a small heat-resistant gratin dish and warm over medium heat.

2 Add the garlic, and sauté slowly until it starts to brown. Remove the garlic, and discard. Stir in the tomatoes and parsley, and cook gently until the tomatoes soften, about 5 minutes.

3 Add the poached egg to the gratin dish. Sprinkle generously with Parmesan cheese, and place in the oven until the cheese has melted, about 1 minute. (Be sure to remove the egg right away, before the yolk has a chance to harden.) Serve right away.

Serves 1

2 teaspoons unsalted butter or extra virgin olive oil

½ clove garlic, crushed

2 ripe Roma tomatoes, chopped

2 tablespoons minced fresh parsley

1 egg, poached

Grated imported Parmesan cheese

Flan des Carottes

CARROT FLAN

Sweet, custardy, and very colorful: a distinctive and delicious dish, indeed.

1 Heat the milk in a large saucepan. Add the carrots, nutmeg, ginger, salt, and pepper, and simmer gently until the carrots are cooked through, about 10 minutes.

2 Remove the carrot mixture from the heat and let cool for about 10 minutes. Puree in a mouli mill, blender, or food processor. Transfer to a mixing bowl and stir in the eggs and cream.

3 Heat the oven to 400°. Grease a 12-inch gratin dish or four 4-inch individual ramekins. Pour the carrot mixture into the gratin dish or distribute it evenly among the ramekins.

4 Place the gratin dish or ramekins inside a larger baking dish, and pour hot water into the outer dish until it rises ⅔ of the way up the sides of the gratin or ramekins. Bake for 30 minutes or until a knife inserted in the center of the flan tests clean. Check the water level during baking, adding more as necessary.

5 Remove the flan from the water bath, and let cool on a rack. Invert the flan onto a serving dish, and serve at room temperature.

Serves 4

1½ cups milk

1 pound carrots, peeled and thinly sliced

Pinch ground nutmeg

Pinch ground ginger

Salt and white pepper to taste

4 eggs, lightly beaten

½ cup heavy cream

risotto, gnocchi, polenta, and pasta

I wonder why certain dishes keep their cultural identity centuries after they've become assimilated into other cuisines; pasta (Italian) is popular in Provence, where polenta (Italian), too, is not unknown. Much of the gnocchi (Italian) served in Siena is made with flour, in a style that in Nice (France) is called Niçoise. As a first course in Florence, you can order crepes (French). And if you have a craving for couscous (Moroccan), you can take care of it far north of Tangier, in Aix-en-Provence or Antibes.

It wasn't a warm welcome, and if I hadn't been so hungry, I would've walked away. But I was willing to trade some pride for a decent meal and hoped that the barter would work in my favor.

The welcome went like this: "*Una* sola?" ("But no one eats alone!!") The welcomer, the waitress, was a girl I would have called tacky if she'd been in my junior high gym class, which means she was enviably endowed and not very shy about it. She wore a black dress like a skin graft and stiletto heels, which were no impediment; she stomped to a table. "*Ecco,*" she said, slamming down a menu—"Here."

A couple sat at the next table, and a man joined them shortly. It was a tight squeeze, so he was actually sitting *with* me. He tried to bring me into the conversation, in Italian. Hopeless. Then in French. Better, but not by much. He shrugged, then devoted himself to his friends. I waited for "her" to return. When she did, unaccountably, I gave my order in Spanish.

The man at the next table grabbed my arm. "*¿Habla Español? ¡Hablo Español!* Now," he went on, in Spanish, "Now we will talk!"

He introduced me to his party, and we all dined together—really together—his fork made regular forays into my risotto. I didn't mind. It seemed less an incursion than a way of including me, a real welcome. And so, after all, the waitress had been right: *No one* (in Florence, anyway) eats alone.

Risotto

Risotto doesn't take much time, but it does take attention. You can't walk off and let it steam, as you would conventional rice. But please don't be daunted by the diligence involved. Some things are worth the trouble, and toothsome risotto, so creamy and good, ranks high among them.

2 tablespoons unsalted butter

1 red onion, chopped

1 cup raw Arborio rice

¼ cup dry white wine

2 cups vegetable broth (page 36), heated to the boiling point

⅓ cup grated imported Parmesan cheese

Salt and freshly ground black pepper to taste

1 Melt the butter in a deep, heavy saucepan over medium heat. Add the onion and sauté until translucent, about 10 minutes. Add the rice and sauté until the grains are coated, about 30 seconds.

2 Pour the wine into the hot broth and add enough of this mixture to the rice to cover the grains by about 2 inches. Stir often over medium heat, adding more liquid as the broth is absorbed, about 20 minutes.

3 When you stir in the last of the liquid, stir in the cheese as well. Cook, continuing to stir, until all of the liquid has been absorbed and the rice is creamy and tender.

4 Remove the rice from the heat and season with salt and pepper. Serve right away.

Serves 4

VARIATION: *Make a little well on the top of each serving and fill with a pool of Sweet Tomato Sauce with Cream (page 30). Top with additional grated Parmesan, if desired.*

Risotto di Peperoni

BELL PEPPER RISOTTO

Mild and sweet, this may be my favorite risotto.

1 Heat the butter in a saucepan. Sauté the shallots and peppers for about 6 minutes, until the peppers have started to soften.

2 Add the rice and stir to mix. Stir in ⅓ (¾ cup) of the broth. Stir again every minute or so, until the liquid is nearly absorbed. Add another ⅓ of the broth, and stir occasionally over medium heat until it has been absorbed, about 20 minutes.

3 Add the last third of the broth. When it's nearly absorbed, stir in the cheese. Continue to simmer until all of the liquid has been absorbed. The rice should be thick and creamy.

4 Season with salt and pepper, and serve right away.

Serves 4

2 tablespoons unsalted butter

2 shallots, minced

½ yellow bell pepper, cored, seeded, and chopped

½ orange bell pepper, cored, seeded, and chopped

1 cup raw Arborio rice

2¼ cups vegetable broth (page 36), heated to the boiling point

⅓ cup grated Fontina or Kasseri cheese

Salt and freshly ground black pepper to taste

Risotto alle Erbe Fresche

RISOTTO WITH FRESH HERBS

If you can bear to stand over a hot stove in the summer, this is the risotto for that time of year.

1 Melt the butter in a deep, heavy saucepan over medium heat. Add the onion and sauté until translucent, about 10 minutes. Add the mint, basil, oregano, and parsley and stir well to combine. Add the rice and sauté until the grains are coated, about 30 seconds.

2 Pour the wine into the hot broth and add enough of this mixture to the rice to cover the grains by about 2 inches. Stir constantly, over medium heat, adding more liquid as it is absorbed, about 20–40 minutes.

3 When you stir in the last of the liquid, stir in the cheese as well. Cook, continuing to stir, until all of the liquid has been absorbed and the rice is creamy and tender.

4 Remove the rice from the heat and season with salt and freshly ground pepper. Serve right away.

Serves 4

VARIATION: *Make a well in the top of each portion and fill with a pool of Sweet Tomato Sauce with Cream (page 30). Sprinkle with additional grated cheese, if desired.*

2 tablespoons unsalted butter

1 red onion, chopped

2 tablespoons finely minced fresh mint

2 tablespoons finely minced fresh basil

2 tablespoons finely minced fresh oregano

2 tablespoons finely minced fresh parsley

1 cup raw Arborio rice

¼ cup dry white wine

2 cups vegetable broth (page 36), heated to the boiling point

½ cup grated Fontina cheese

Salt and freshly ground black pepper to taste

Risotto con Piselli Verdi

RISOTTO WITH FRESH GREEN PEAS

Saffron is a splendid companion to fresh peas and Parmesan.

1 Heat together the butter and olive oil in a deep, heavy saucepan over medium heat. When the butter has melted, add the shallots and sauté until soft, about 6 minutes. Add the rice and sauté until the grains are coated, about 30 seconds.

2 Pour the wine into the hot broth and add enough of this mixture to the rice to cover the grains by about 2 inches. Stir often over medium heat, adding more liquid as it is absorbed, about 20 minutes.

3 Just before adding the last of the liquid, sprinkle in the saffron powder. Stir in the rest of the liquid, the peas, and the cheese. Cook, continuing to stir often, until the rice is creamy and soft. The entire process should take 30–40 minutes.

4 Remove the rice from the heat and season with salt and pepper. Serve right away.

Serves 4

1 tablespoon unsalted butter

1 tablespoon extra virgin olive oil

2 shallots, minced

1 cup raw Arborio rice

¼ cup dry white wine

2 cups vegetable broth (page 36), heated to the boiling point

½ teaspoon saffron powder

1 cup shelled fresh green peas

⅓ cup grated imported Parmesan cheese

Salt and freshly ground black pepper to taste

Risotto con Menta

RISOTTO WITH MINT

Mint turns wonderfully mellow in the presence of Parmesan.

1 Melt the butter in a deep, heavy saucepan over medium heat. Add the shallots and sauté until translucent, about 10 minutes. Add the mint and stir to combine. Stir in the rice and sauté until the grains are coated, about 30 seconds.

2 Pour the wine into the hot broth and add enough of this mixture to the rice to cover the grains by about 2 inches. Stir often at medium heat, adding more liquid as the broth is absorbed, about 20 minutes.

3 When you stir in the last of the liquid, stir in the cheese as well. Cook, continuing to stir, until all of the liquid has been absorbed and the rice is creamy and tender.

4 Remove the rice from the heat and season with salt and freshly ground pepper. Serve right away.

Serves 4

2 tablespoons unsalted butter

2 shallots, minced

2 tablespoons finely minced fresh mint

1 cup raw Arborio rice

¼ cup dry white wine

2 cups vegetable broth (page 36), heated to the boiling point

½ cup grated imported Parmesan cheese

Salt and freshly ground black pepper to taste

Risotto à la Niçoise

RICE WITH TOMATO, OLIVES, AND PINE NUTS

This is truly a border special, combining the Tuscan way with rice (simmering in an open pot), with a Niçoise signature mix (olives, tomato, and saffron). Serve it alongside a simple frittata.

1 Heat the olive oil and sauté the scallions until soft, about 7 minutes. Add the rice and stir until glossy, about 30 seconds.

2 Stir in the tomatoes and the hot water or broth, the saffron, and a few grindings of black pepper. Cover tightly.

3 Reduce the heat and cook for 15 minutes. Toss in the olives, pine nuts, and raisins, without stirring. Cover again, and cook until the rice absorbs all of the liquid, about 10 minutes longer. Turn off the heat.

4 Let rest, covered, 10 minutes before serving.

Serves 6

NOTE: *To toast the pine nuts, heat the oven or toaster oven to 425°. Spread the pine nuts on a baking sheet in a single layer, and bake until golden, 4–5 minutes. Watch carefully to make sure they don't burn.*

3 tablespoons extra virgin olive oil

2 scallions, white part only, minced

1 cup raw medium-grain white rice

1 cup ripe peeled, seeded, drained, chopped tomatoes, or 1 cup canned or boxed imported Italian tomatoes

1½ cups water or vegetable broth (page 36), heated to the boiling point

Pinch powdered saffron

Freshly ground black pepper to taste

¼ cup chopped pitted Greek-style black olives

¼ cup pine nuts, lightly toasted (see note below)

¼ cup raisins

Risotto al Prezzemolo

PARSLEY RICE

Very simple, very good.

1 Cook the rice according to package directions. Let it rest, covered, for 10 minutes.

2 In an earthenware mixing bowl, place the butter, parsley, and cheese. Add the hot cooked rice, and toss well. Season with salt and freshly ground black pepper. Serve immediately, or at room temperature.

Serves 6

1 cup raw medium-grain white rice

1 tablespoon unsalted butter

1 large bunch parsley, minced

¼ cup grated imported Parmesan cheese

Salt and freshly ground black pepper to taste

Riz au Citron

RICE WITH A HINT OF LEMON

A chef in Aix-en-Provence served the perkiest white rice, garnished with lemon peel and Parmesan. *Le voilà!*

1 Cook the rice according to package directions. Meanwhile, in a large earthenware mixing bowl, combine the butter, egg, lemon peel, Parmesan, and chives.

2 When the rice is done, let it sit, covered, 10 minutes. Then transfer to the mixing bowl and toss with the rest of the ingredients. Season with salt and pepper, and serve right away.

Serves 6

1 cup raw medium-grain white rice

1 tablespoon unsalted butter

1 egg, well beaten

½ tablespoon finely minced lemon zest

2 tablespoons grated imported Parmesan cheese

2 tablespoons minced fresh chives

Salt and freshly ground black pepper to taste

The subject was antipasto (the French couple wanted to order it for one; the Italian head waiter said it was only prepared for two or more), but the argument wasn't about food; it was a border dispute. They insulted him, compounding the effect by doing it in French. Clearly, he understood French, or he wouldn't have turned so red or bellowed so loudly. And clearly, they understood Italian, or they wouldn't have known exactly what to bellow back. That they understood each other perfectly was the whole point: There could be no mistake—each spoke his own language, not because he couldn't speak the other's, but because he *wouldn't*. A curious posture, especially in the case of the couple who'd gone out of the way, from France to Florence, to eat Italian food.

Fortunately, many dishes such as pasta, crepes, gnocchi, and pizza cross the border with more grace than some individuals.

Gnocchi à la Romaine

SEMOLINA GNOCCHI

There is no definitive gnocchi; order gnocchi in either Italy or France and you may get a dish made with potatoes, pumpkin, puff pastry, semolina, or ricotta cheese. It may come baked and drenched in sauce, or boiled, buttered, and dusted with Parmesan or *pecorino*. Here is the semolina version, which, while named "Romaine" for "Rome" turns up all over Nice.

Serve this gnocchi simply, as follows, or top it with pesto or the tomato sauce of your choice.

4¼ cups milk

Pinch salt

Pinch of nutmeg

1⅔ cup fine semolina flour

1 cup finely grated imported Parmesan cheese

4 tablespoons butter

2 egg yolks, lightly beaten

1 Bring the milk to a boil and add the salt and nutmeg. Beat in the semolina, and cook 3 to 4 minutes, until the mixture is very thick.

2 Take the pot off the heat and vigorously stir in half of the grated Parmesan, 1 tablespoon of the butter, and the egg yolks.

3 Turn the mixture out onto a lightly buttered work surface or a marble slab. Let it cool. Meanwhile, melt the remaining butter. Heat the oven to 425°.

4 When the mixture has cooled spread the dough to a thickness of ⅓ inch. Use a liqueur glass or small cookie cutter to cut it into rounds 2 inches in diameter.

5 Place the gnocchi in a greased gratin dish. Pour the melted butter on top, and sprinkle generously with the remaining Parmesan. Bake briefly until the cheese is bubbly.

Serves 6

VARIATION: *Top the gnocchi with the pesto on page 26 or the tomato sauce on page 28.*

Gnocchi di Patate

These delightfully dense potato dumplings are so chewy and good in a blanket of béchamel, I had to battle the urge to bury my face in the bowl the first time I had them served that way.

1 Put the potatoes in a medium saucepan and add water to cover. Bring to a boil, and let simmer until the potatoes are cooked through, about 40 minutes. Remove the potatoes with a slotted spoon and let them drain thoroughly on paper towels. Pat them dry before proceeding to the next step. Or heat the oven to 425° and bake the potatoes until done, about an hour. Peel them and proceed as follows.

2 Puree the potatoes with a mouli mill, an egg beater, or an electric hand mixer. Transfer the puree to a mixing bowl.

3 Using a wooden spoon, beat the egg yolks, half the flour, and a pinch of salt into the potatoes. Stir in as much additional flour as you need to make a dough you can handle. Knead the dough until smooth.

4 Divide the dough into portions the size of a tangerine. Roll each on a floured surface into a rope about ⅔ inch thick. Cut the rope into segments about an inch long.

5 Press the gnocchi with the tines of a fork to make indentations, which will cradle the topping.

1¾ pounds potatoes, peeled and quartered or left whole, for baking

2 egg yolks, beaten

¾ cups all-purpose flour, approximately

Salt to taste

¼ cup grated imported Parmesan cheese

¼ cup unsalted butter, melted

Freshly ground black pepper to taste

6 Bring a large pot of lightly salted water to a boil. Add the gnocchi, and cook until they rise to the surface.

7 Remove with a slotted spoon, and let them drain in a colander.

8 Transfer to an earthenware serving bowl, and toss with grated Parmesan, melted butter, and salt and pepper.

Serves 6

N O T E : *You can make gnocchi with boiled or baked potatoes. Boiling is faster, but gnocchi made with baked potatoes are firmer, and less prone to burst at the simmering stage. I prefer organic russet potatoes, which tend to be silkier and more robust than the rest.*

Pumpkin Gnocchi

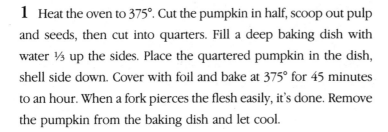

1 Heat the oven to 375°. Cut the pumpkin in half, scoop out pulp and seeds, then cut into quarters. Fill a deep baking dish with water ⅓ up the sides. Place the quartered pumpkin in the dish, shell side down. Cover with foil and bake at 375° for 45 minutes to an hour. When a fork pierces the flesh easily, it's done. Remove the pumpkin from the baking dish and let cool.

2 Spoon the pumpkin out of the shell and into a large mixing bowl. Mash with a fork until it is the consistency of mashed potatoes. Add flour ½ cup at a time, mashing to blend it with the pumpkin, until you have a dough you can handle.

3 Take a golf ball–sized piece of dough in your hands and roll it into a log shape, about 2½–3 inches long. Cut in half and indent the center of each half with your thumb. (The indentation will hold the topping.) Place on lightly floured wax paper. Continue until you've used all the dough.

4 Bring a pot of lightly salted water to a boil. Add the gnocchi. As soon as they rise to the surface, remove them with a slotted spoon, drain well, then place in a warm, covered serving dish.

5 Sprinkle the cinnamon and sugar into the butter, toss with the gnocchi, then toss with Parmesan cheese. Serve immediately.

Serves 6–8

One 2-pound pumpkin (use only fresh pumpkin—canned pulp is too watery)

3 cups (approximately) unbleached flour

½ teaspoon ground cinnamon

Pinch sugar

½ cup butter, melted

⅓ cup grated imported Parmesan cheese

Gnocchi con Spinaci

SPINACH-RICOTTA DUMPLINGS

While many Florentines have become justly famous—Dante, Michelangelo, Donatello, Giotto—the name of one inspired Florentine has been lost to history: the one who first combined spinach, ricotta, and nutmeg, the city's culinary signature and a most excellent filling for calzone, crepes, savory tortes, frittatas, and, as follows, these gnocchi, or dumplings.

1 In a mixing bowl, stir together the spinach, egg, ricotta cheese, ½ cup Parmesan cheese, mozzarella cheese, nutmeg, and flour. Mix until well combined.

2 Roughly 1 tablespoon at a time, shape the mixture into balls. Place on a plate, cover, and refrigerate 5 hours or more.

3 Heat the oven to 300°. Bring lightly salted water to a boil in a kettle or deep saucepan. Boil the dumplings no more than 6 at a time until they float to the surface, about 5 minutes. Remove with a slotted spoon, and let drain on paper towels.

4 When all have been cooked, transfer the dumplings to a well-buttered baking dish, cover with foil, and reheat in the oven for 10 minutes. Place the 1 tablespoon butter in the bottom of a large nonmetallic mixing bowl. Add the hot dumplings, and stir with a wooden spoon to coat evenly. Add tomato sauce and stir again. Serve immediately, passing grated Parmesan on the side.

Serves 6

One 8-ounce package frozen chopped spinach, thawed and squeezed dry

1 egg, lightly beaten

1 pound ricotta cheese (low fat, if desired)

½ cup grated imported Parmesan cheese

½ cup finely shredded mozzarella cheese

Pinch ground nutmeg

½ cup semolina flour

1 tablespoon unsalted butter

¾ cup Sweet Tomato Sauce with Cream (page 30)

Grated imported Parmesan cheese

Florence inspires great pride in humanity, and some befuddlement. It's the cradle of the Renaissance; the birthplace of Giotto, Dante, Michelangelo, and Brunelleschi; a town whose many treasures testify to the generosity and good taste of that most ardent patron of the arts, Cosimo de' Medici.

Yet to find the city altogether enchanting, it helps to be a bit ignorant.

For example, the Michelin guide would have you charmed by the Piazza della Signoria—where stands a replica of Michelangelo's *David,* and another of *Perseus,* by Cellini. But I happen to know that a man was eaten there.

And the Boboli Gardens—lovely to some—look sinister to me. I know that lovesick Princess Violante Beatrice of Bavaria was married there to the philandering Ferdinando de' Medici on a day so cold that two members of their procession froze to death.

And even the Duomo—Brunelleschi's masterpiece, a pinnacle of Western architecture—becomes complicated once you know that, from the pulpit, the zealot Savonarola incited riots and kindled his "bonfire of the vanities," wasting untold volumes of books and works of art. Knowing this, you might be a bit distracted from Brunelleschi's accomplishment. But then again, you might be accused of being a bad sport.

Is it ironic that one city should spawn such extremes—extreme refinement on the one hand, and gross depravity on the other? Or is it only natural that a place that fostered the humanities should be so utterly human?

Polenta

In a rare reversal of customary culinary migration, this began as an American dish. Some itinerant Italians took it home, where it caught on in a way it never has over here—perhaps because the Italians call it polenta, while we insist on bluntly descriptive, wholly unappetizing "cornmeal mush."

4 cups lightly salted water

1 cup cornmeal

Salt and freshly ground black pepper to taste

1½ cups tomato sauce of your choice

Grated imported Parmesan, pecorino, or Fontina cheese

1 In a large saucepan, bring the lightly salted water to a boil.

2 Sprinkle in the cornmeal (the Italians say to let it flow through your fingers so that it falls in like rain). Let it simmer, stirring constantly, until it's thick enough to pull away from the side of the pot and stand on its own, 30–40 minutes.

3 Distribute the polenta among 6 soup bowls and serve topped with tomato sauce and cheese.

Serves 6

Polenta al Forno

BAKED POLENTA

What a treat to bite into these squares, crisp on the top and soft in the center.

1 Preheat the oven to 375°. Prepare polenta according to recipe. Turn the polenta out onto a cookie sheet or marble slab, and spread to a thickness of about an inch. Let it cool.

2 Cut it into squares, brush lightly with olive oil, and bake at 375° until a golden crust forms on top, about 15 minutes.

3 Serve the squares topped with Simple Tomato Sauce or Mushroom Cream Sauce.

Serves 6

1 recipe polenta (page 133)

2 teaspoons extra virgin olive oil

1 recipe Simple Tomato Sauce (page 27) or 1 recipe Mushroom Cream Sauce (page 31)

Farinata di Noci

POLENTA WITH WALNUTS

Hearty and rich, especially welcome in wintertime.

1 Bring the water to a boil, and sprinkle in the cornmeal (the Italians tell you to toss the cornmeal so it falls like rain).

2 Simmer on low heat, stirring often to prevent lumps.

3 Meanwhile, heat the olive oil and sauté the walnuts and rosemary just until well coated. Be careful not to burn the walnuts.

4 When the polenta has thickened, after 30 minutes or so, stir in the walnut mixture. Keep cooking until the polenta is thick enough to stand on its own when pulled away from the sides of the pot, about 10 minutes more. Serve hot as it is or topped with the sauce of your choice.

Serves 6

4 cups lightly salted water

1 cup cornmeal

1 tablespoon extra virgin olive oil

¼ cup coarsely crushed walnuts

1 tablespoon minced rosemary

Salt and freshly ground black pepper to taste

Farinata Giallo

POLENTA WITH TOMATO

Cornmeal is called *granturco* in Italy, for the Turks who introduced corn to the Continent. Here it's prepared with tomato paste
and powdered with *pecorino* cheese.

1 Heat the olive oil in a saucepan and sauté the onion until soft
and translucent, about 7 minutes.

2 Add the tomato paste.

3 Stir in the water. Bring to a simmer.

4 Sprinkle in the cornmeal (the Italians say to let it flow through
your fingers so that it falls like rain). Let it simmer, stirring constantly, until it's thick enough to pull away from the side of the pot
and stand on its own, about 40 minutes.

5 Transfer to an earthenware bowl, sprinkle *unsparingly* with
grated cheese, and serve right away.

Serves 6

1 tablespoon extra virgin olive oil

1 small white onion, chopped

1 tablespoon tomato paste

4 cups lightly salted water

1 cup cornmeal

Grated imported pecorino or Parmesan cheese

Pasta con Uova
e Formaggi

PASTA WITH SMOKED MOZZARELLA, EGGS, AND CREAM

This may be the richest dish in my repertoire, so, naturally, one of the best.

1 Soften the butter in a mixing bowl, beating with a fork until it's smooth.

2 In another bowl beat together the eggs, egg yolks, and half the grated Parmesan.

3 Cook the pasta al dente, according to package directions. Drain the pasta in a colander. Return the cooking pot to the stove, and put the butter into it. Toss in the pasta, then add the egg mixture, crème fraîche, and smoked cheese.

4 Season with salt and pepper. Toss with the remaining Parmesan, and serve immediately.

Serves 6

2 tablespoons unsalted butter

3 eggs

3 egg yolks

1/2 cup grated imported Parmesan cheese

1 pound dry tagliatelle or fettuccine

1/4 cup crème fraîche (page 25)

1/2 cup shredded smoked mozzarella cheese

Salt and freshly ground black pepper to taste

Pasta con Pesto / Spaghetti au Pistou

~~~

PASTA WITH BASIL, PINE NUTS, AND CHEESE

This is the Italian version of pistou (page 26). Serve it on pasta, polenta, or gnocchi.

1 With a mortar and pestle, grind together the garlic and basil. Then grind in the olive oil and half of the Parmesan cheese. Transfer the paste from the mortar to another bowl.

2 In the mortar, grind the pine nuts, then blend into the other paste. Season with salt and pepper.

3 Cook the pasta according to package directions. Toss with the butter, pesto, and the rest of the Parmesan cheese.

Serves 6

3 large cloves garlic

10 leaves basil, minced

2 tablespoons extra virgin olive oil

½ cup grated imported Parmesan cheese

½ cup pine nuts

Salt and freshly ground black pepper to taste

1 pound dry pasta

1 tablespoon unsalted butter

Pasta alla Caprese

PASTA WITH FRESH MOZZARELLA, BASIL, AND TOMATOES

The finest fresh mozzarella melts on the tongue; try it once, and you'll forsake forever the plastic-wrapped kind more commonly found in the dairy case. Here its subtle flavor balances the strident taste of basil.

1 Heat the olive oil in a small skillet. Add the garlic and sauté until it starts to brown. Remove the garlic and discard.

2 Cook the pasta according to package directions.

3 Meanwhile, toss the tomatoes into the olive oil, and sauté until they start to break down, about 5 minutes. Remove from the heat, and transfer to a small mixing bowl. Stir in the mozzarella and basil.

4 Drain the pasta and distribute it evenly among 4 serving bowls. Top each with equal portions of the tomato mixture. Season with black pepper, and sprinkle with Parmesan cheese, if desired. Serve immediately.

Serves 4

2 tablespoons extra virgin olive oil of the best quality

1 clove garlic, sliced

12 ounces dry pasta (angel hair, spaghetti, tagliatelle, farfalle)

4 large ripe tomatoes, peeled, seeded, drained, and chopped

8 ounces fresh mozzarella, cut into bite-size pieces

6 leaves basil, finely minced

Freshly ground black pepper to taste

Grated imported Parmesan cheese (optional)

Pasta della Contadina

COUNTRY GARDEN SAUCE WITH PASTA

A simple sauce that makes good use of the bounty of summer.

1 Heat the olive oil and gently sauté the onion, garlic, and carrot until everything is soft, about 10 minutes.

2 Add the tomatoes, basil, and parsley. Continue to cook until the tomatoes break down into a sauce, about 10 minutes more. Season with salt and pepper.

3 Cook the pasta al dente, according to package directions.

4 Drain the pasta, distribute evenly among 4–6 serving bowls, top with the sauce, and sprinkle with cheese.

Serves 4–6

2 tablespoons extra virgin olive oil

1 large white onion, chopped

3 cloves garlic, crushed and minced

1 large carrot, peeled and chopped

2 pounds ripe tomatoes, peeled, seeded, and chopped, or 2 pounds canned or boxed imported Italian tomatoes, chopped

¼ cup minced fresh basil

1 bunch parsley, minced

Salt and freshly ground black pepper to taste

1 pound dry or fresh tagliatelle

Grated imported pecorino, Asiago, or Parmesan cheese to taste

Tabbouleh à la Provençale

Tabbouleh is typically made with coarse bulgur wheat. But in southern France, they make a silky version with couscous.

1 Heat the olive oil in a wide saucepan, and sauté the onion and garlic until the onion is soft and translucent, 7–10 minutes.

2 Add the roasted peppers and sauté, stirring often, about 20 minutes. Stir in the raisins and the chick-peas.

3 Add the water, cover, and bring to a boil. Stir in the couscous, cover, and bring to a second boil.

4 Turn off the heat and let the couscous sit, tightly covered, for 10 minutes.

5 Uncover, fluff the couscous with a fork, and toss with the mint and 1 tablespoon olive oil. Season with salt and pepper. Let cool to room temperature before serving.

Serves 4

N O T E : *To roast and peel peppers, split in half lengthwise, and remove the seeds and core. Place skin side up on a broiler pan and broil until the skin is evenly charred. Transfer from the sheet to a paper bag, close, and let steam for 10 to 15 minutes. Open the bag and let the remaining steam escape. When the peppers are cool enough to handle, the skin should peel away easily.*

2 tablespoons extra virgin olive oil

1 small white onion, coarsely chopped

1 clove garlic, crushed and minced

1 red bell pepper, roasted, peeled, and chopped (see note below)

1 yellow bell pepper, roasted, peeled, and chopped

1 orange bell pepper, roasted, peeled, and chopped

¼ cup golden raisins

½ cup canned or freshly cooked and drained chick-peas

1 cup water

¾ cup raw couscous

2 tablespoons finely minced fresh mint

1 tablespoon extra virgin olive oil of the best quality

Salt and freshly ground black pepper to taste

Oncle Jean

BAKED DUMPLINGS WITH PUMPKIN, CHEESE, AND RICE

Who was Uncle Jean? Did he create this dish? Or was it named for him because he put away such prodigious portions of these great baked dumplings? Sadly, culinary history yields no clues on this question. We could scratch our heads for centuries if we add to that enigma the question, Why, when made with spinach instead of squash, is the dish called *boussotou?*

1 For the dumplings, on a large work surface (a marble slab is ideal for this) measure out the flour. Make a well in the center and add the olive oil, water, egg, and salt. Gather it all together with your hands, and knead. If the dough is too dry to knead, add more water, bit by bit, until it's pliable. Knead until smooth and elastic.

It's easier, of course, to make the dough in a food processor. Combine all of the dumpling ingredients in the work bowl, fitted with the metal blade. Process until the dough forms a ball and becomes pliable, adjusting flour or water as necessary. Turn out onto a work surface and knead until smooth and elastic.

2 Shape the dough into a ball and let it rest on the work surface, covered with a damp kitchen towel, about 1 hour.

3 Cut into 2 portions. Roll each portion out into a thin (⅛-inch) sheet. Cut into rounds, 4 inches in diameter.

DUMPLINGS

2 cups unbleached flour

¼ cup extra virgin olive oil

¼ cup water

1 egg, lightly beaten

Pinch salt

FILLING

4 cups diced pumpkin or any variety winter squash, or 2 cups canned pumpkin

2 tablespoons extra virgin olive oil

1 white onion, chopped

1 clove garlic, minced

2 eggs, lightly beaten

2 cups cooked white rice

1 cup grated imported Parmesan cheese

Salt and freshly ground black pepper to taste

4 For the filling: If you're using fresh pumpkin, bring to a boil enough lightly salted water to cover the diced pumpkin or squash. Boil until soft. Puree with a mouli mill or a food processor, taking care not to liquefy.

5 Heat the olive oil, and sauté the onion and garlic until the onion turns soft and translucent, about 7 minutes.

6 In a mixing bowl, combine the onion and garlic, eggs, rice, pureed pumpkin or squash, and grated cheese. Season with salt and pepper. Heat the oven to 425°.

7 Place a heaping teaspoon of the squash mixture in the center of each pasta round, and fold over into a half-moon shape. Wet your fingers, and press along the seam to seal.

8 Place on a large lightly oiled gratin dish. Bake until golden, about 15 minutes. Serve right away.

Serves 6

VARIATION: *Use 2 packed cups cooked, chopped spinach, well drained, instead of the pumpkin or squash.*

It was so hot in Aix-en-Provence that ice cubes promptly melted. It was hot in Aix, "But not as hot as where we're going,'" a strident American told a griping companion.

They took the table next to mine—two boys with only one thing in common: crew cuts. The loud one was beefy and wore those reflector shades preferred by small-town sheriffs. The whiner was scrawny and squinted into the sun. "Yeah, I know," the skinny one said. His voice cracked. "Don't remind me." Then he slumped in his seat.

If it hadn't been so hot I might have told him to cheer up. "It's France!" I would've cried. *"Joie de vivre—esprit de corps!"* and all that.

But spirit was as futile as ice in that heat. I just couldn't put it across.

His attitude, I learned shortly, was suffering from more than the sun. It was the end of his shore leave, and when he returned to Marseilles, his ship would be going to the Persian Gulf. He'd caught wind of the rumors of war, and so there he was, sweltering in the summer sun and chilled through with fear.

It cooled off toward evening, and I saw them again, on the steps of the museum. They asked me the way to the Burger King. Ordinarily, I'd cringe. But I couldn't blame them for wanting a taste of the home that would shortly be even farther away.

In fact, Aix, a tiny haven for refugees from the Middle and Far East, is full of people hungry for something from a home somewhere else. And so it's full of Thai and Chinese restaurants, as well as cafés serving couscous, pilafs, and stuffed grape leaves. There are burger chains, too. Considered in that context, I couldn't object.

Dolmades

STUFFED GRAPE LEAVES

If you didn't know where you were, you'd find few clues in Aix—
not in the falafel vendor (wearing a fez) or in the cases full of feta,
phyllo, and dolmades.

1 In a large saucepan, heat the olive oil and sauté the onions
over medium-low heat until very soft, about 40 minutes.

2 Add the currants, pine nuts, cumin, cinnamon, allspice, salt,
and rice, and stir until well combined.

3 Pour in 1⅓ cups of the broth, cover, boil, and lower to a
simmer. Cook, tightly covered, until all the liquid is absorbed,
about 20 minutes.

4 Place a teaspoon or so of the filling in the center of each leaf.

5 Fold the sides over the stuffing, like an envelope. Hold in your
palm and squeeze each, to seal.

6 Place all of the dolmades seam side down in a large skillet.

7 Combine the lemon juice with the remaining broth. Pour into
the skillet, to about halfway up the layers of dolmades.

8 Weigh down with a heavy heat-resistant plate.

9 Simmer until very soft, about 40 minutes. Let cool; refrigerate
for at least 3 hours. Serve chilled or at room temperature.

Serves 6–8

⅓ cup extra virgin olive oil

3 cups chopped white onions

¼ cup currants

¼ cup pine nuts

2 teaspoons ground cumin

1 teaspoon ground cinnamon

½ teaspoon allspice

1 teaspoon salt

⅔ cup raw long-grain white rice

2⅓ cups vegetable broth (page 36)

1 jar grape leaves (about 40 count), drained and well rinsed

Juice of 1 lemon

pizza, savory tortes, crepes, and such

There's a bakery in Florence that defies you to leave town. It turns out an apparently infinite variety of little pizzas and displays them in such an appetizing array that even the potato pizza looks good. Moreover, it is good, so good that mustering the resolve to pack for home is impossible without swearing on something very dear to you that you'll be back for more.

Pizza

From Avignon to Siena, everything that *is* is bound to turn up on a pizza. Anything goes. And so to be doctrinaire about pizza is to miss the point.

1 In a small bowl, combine the yeast and water. In a large earthenware bowl, combine the flour and salt. Or put the flour and salt into the work bowl of a food processor, and combine.

2 Make a well in the flour mixture, and pour in the dissolved yeast and the olive oil. Or if using a food processor, add dissolved yeast and oil while motor is running.

3 Stir or process until your dough is pliable, adding more flour if necessary. Turn out onto a lightly floured surface, and knead until smooth and springy, 10–15 minutes. Transfer to a lightly floured bowl, and cover with a damp cloth. Let rise in a warm, draft-free spot until doubled, about 2 hours.

4 Punch down the dough, and divide into 6 portions. Shape each into a ball and let rest, covered, about 10 minutes. Roll out each portion into a circle, 6 inches in diameter, cover, and let rest again for an hour. Heat the oven to 425°.

5 Brush lightly with extra virgin olive oil and top with one of the following toppings (quantities given are for individual pizzas). Bake until the crust is crisp and golden, about 15–20 minutes.

(continued on next page)

CRUST

½ package active dry yeast

1 cup warm water

2 cups unbleached flour (more as needed)

2 teaspoons salt

1 tablespoon olive oil

Potatoes: 1 thinly sliced peeled russet potato, sautéed in 1 teaspoon each unsalted butter and extra virgin olive oil, then sprinkled with 1 teaspoon minced fresh rosemary and coarse salt to taste.

Tomatoes: 1 thinly sliced ripe unpeeled tomato, sautéed in 1 teaspoon extra virgin olive oil with ½ clove garlic, sliced, and 2 tablespoons of fresh basil.

Cheese: ¼ cup mozzarella cheese topped with 1 thinly sliced fresh tomato that's been sautéed with ½ clove garlic and fresh basil, and sprinkled with ¼ cup grated imported Parmesan or *pecorino* cheese.

Zucchini: 1 thinly sliced zucchini sautéed with ½ clove garlic, sliced, in 1 teaspoon extra virgin olive oil. Discard the garlic and drain well before putting on the dough. Sprinkle with coarse salt and 1 tablespoon finely minced fresh basil.

Asparagus: 4 steamed asparagus tips sautéed in 1 teaspoon each unsalted butter and extra virgin olive oil with ½ clove garlic, sliced. Discard garlic before using as a topping. Sprinkle with ¼ cup grated imported Parmesan.

Cheese and mushrooms: ¼ cup shredded mozzarella cheese topped with 4 thinly sliced button mushrooms that have been sautéed in 1 teaspoon each unsalted butter and extra virgin olive oil with ½ clove garlic, sliced, and ¼ cup fresh parsley. Sprinkle with 2 tablespoons finely minced basil.

Spinach Calzone

In Florence you'll find calzone made with crust that's thin and soft like pita bread or flour tortillas or with crust that's toothsome and dense. This is the thicker version.

1 For the crust, in a large mixing bowl, stir together the yeast, sugar, water, and 1 cup of the flour. Let stand until foamy, about 10 minutes. You can also combine them in the work bowl of a food processor, using the metal blade.

2 Whisk together the milk and egg, and add to the yeast mixture. Stir in the salt and add the remaining flour, ½ cup at a time, until the dough is stiff enough to handle.

3 Turn out onto a lightly floured surface (preferably a marble slab), and knead until smooth and elastic, about 5 minutes.

4 Transfer to a lightly oiled earthenware bowl. Cover with a damp towel, and let rise in a warm place until doubled, about 2 hours.

5 Punch down the dough and turn out onto a lightly floured surface. Knead to get rid of air pockets, about 5 minutes.

6 Cut into 6 pieces of equal size.

(continued on next page)

CRUST

1 package active dry yeast

1 tablespoon sugar

¼ cup warm water

3¾ cups unbleached flour

1 cup warm milk

1 egg, beaten

2 teaspoons salt

7 For the filling, in an earthenware mixing bowl, combine the spinach, ricotta, mozzarella, Parmesan, tomatoes, nutmeg, and salt and pepper. Stir well.

8 To prepare each calzone, heat the oven to 425°. Sprinkle a baking sheet with cornmeal. Pat out 1 piece of dough and roll into a round about ¼ inch thick. Place ⅙ of the filling in the center, and fold the top over, sealing with the tines of a fork.

9 Pierce the dough in several places with the fork. Make an egg wash by beating together the egg whites and a few drops of water. Brush the calzone with the egg wash.

10 Place the calzone on the prepared baking sheet and cover with a towel. Let rest 10 minutes. Then bake at 425° until the crust is golden-brown, about 20 minutes.

11 Repeat for the rest of the dough and filling.

Makes 6 calzone

SPINACH FILLING

Two 8-ounce packages frozen chopped spinach, thawed and squeezed dry

1 pound ricotta cheese, drained if runny

½ cup shredded mozzarella cheese

¼ cup grated imported Parmesan cheese

2 medium ripe tomatoes, peeled, seeded, well drained, and chopped

Pinch ground nutmeg

Salt and freshly ground black pepper to taste

Cornmeal

3 egg whites

Tomato and Basil Calzone

1 Prepare calzone dough as described in steps 1–6, page 149.

2 In a medium skillet, heat the olive oil. Sauté the garlic until it starts to brown. Remove the garlic and discard it.

3 In a mixing bowl, combine the tomatoes, mozzarella, Parmesan, and basil.

4 Roll the 6 portions of dough out into rounds, distribute the tomato mixture evenly over the dough. Brush the tomato topping with the flavored olive oil. Fold the dough over and seal with the tines of a fork. Proceed as directed in steps 9–11, page 150.

Makes 6 calzone

1 recipe calzone dough (page 149)

¼ cup extra virgin olive oil

1 clove garlic, crushed and minced

8 medium ripe tomatoes, peeled, seeded, and chopped, or 2 cups drained and chopped canned or boxed imported Italian tomatoes

¾ cup shredded mozzarella cheese

¼ cup grated imported Parmesan cheese

¼ cup minced fresh basil

Forget the riddle of the Sphinx. For me, the far more baffling question is, Why aren't the French fat? How is it that the Japanese raise successive generations of sumo wrestlers on raw fish and rice, while the French, with their well-known penchant for butter and cream, are so svelte?

I thought I had the answer, at breakfast in Aix-en-Provence. A woman of fifty, maybe (*bon chic* most definitely), took a table near mine. Her order was Spartan enough: coffee and bread.

Then I knew I was onto something. She was hollowing out the bread! That's how they do it! They don't really eat! This magical metabolism—it's a myth!

But then she confounded me. She unwrapped one chunk of butter and spread it—*all* of it—on the bread. She ate it, then did the same with the other half.

It gets worse.

She took the little square of chocolate that came with her coffee and stirred it into her cup, along with a sugar cube and about 3 inches of milk. Whole milk.

So maybe it's the way they eat that accounts for it. Not idly, as we often do, to pass the time, but with gusto. Yes, surely, gusto is what does the trick.

Pissaladière

Each *boulangerie* in southern France has its own version of this addictive dish. Some are very simple—just bread strewn with sautéed onions and black olives. Others are much more complicated, such as pastry shells filled, fluted, and baked in a slow oven. This one is my favorite, prepared like pizza—a dense, chewy crust, with a sweet mess of onions melting down into it. The secret to this sensational Pissaladière is sautéeing the onions for a long, long time—40 minutes or more.

Pissaladière, in this case, is a misnomer, since the name refers to the anchovy paste (*pissalta*) that figured in the original.

1 For the crust, in a large earthenware bowl or the work bowl of a food processor, combine the yeast, sugar, water, and 1 cup of the flour. Let rest until the mixture becomes puffy and dotted with small air holes, 5–7 minutes.

2 Mix or process in the salt, and add more flour, ½ cup at a time, until the dough is pliable.

3 Lightly flour a work surface (a marble slab makes kneading much easier), turn the dough out of the bowl, and knead until the dough is smooth and springy, 8–10 minutes. Shape the dough into a ball.

(continued on next page)

CRUST

1 package active dry yeast

2 teaspoons sugar

1 cup warm water

2½ cups (approximately) unbleached flour

2 teaspoons salt

TOPPING

⅓ cup extra virgin olive oil

6 large Spanish onions, thinly sliced

12 Greek-style black olives, pitted and chopped

2 large ripe tomatoes, peeled, seeded, well drained, and chopped (optional)

4 Lightly oil a large earthenware bowl. Place the dough in the bowl, and cover with a damp kitchen towel. Put in a warm, draft-free place. (A gas oven lined with baking stones is ideal for this.) Let rise until doubled, about 1 hour.

5 Punch down the dough, turn out onto a lightly floured surface, and knead again to press out the air bubbles, about 5 minutes.

6 Return to the earthenware bowl, cover, and let rise until doubled, another hour.

7 Lightly oil a 12-inch pizza pan or two 6-inch ceramic or metallic quiche pans. Punch down the dough again and knead it again to get rid of air bubbles, about 5 minutes.

8 With a rolling pin, roll out the dough to fit the pans. Transfer to the prepared pans. Cover with a towel and let rest 15 minutes.

9 For the topping, while the dough is rising for the second time, heat the olive oil in a large, deep skillet.

10 Sauté the onions over low heat, stirring often, until mushy, about 40 minutes.

11 Heat the oven to 400°.

12 Spread the onions over the dough in the pans, then distribute the olives and tomatoes, if using, evenly over the top.

13 Bake 20 minutes. Lower the heat to 375° and bake 10 minutes more, until the crust is golden and crisp. Serve hot.

Serves 6–8

There are two stereotypes about the French that contradict each other. One is that they snub you if you speak their language poorly; the other is that they're nice to you as long as you try. The second, I think, is true. But, while effort might be good for relations, it's often not as effective for communications, as I learned at lunch one day in Aix-en-Provence. There were several savory tortes, and I chose—I thought—one with vegetables and aromatic herbs. But my desire was more keen than my ability to express it. I got lamb pie instead and didn't know it until I'd eaten a huge heaping forkful.

To a palate primed for something more subtle, it was a shock. And while I may have garbled my order, I put over an excellent and most effective gasp; the waitress brought me a glass of water and, shortly, a piece of torte that was more to my taste.

Tourte de Blette

SWISS CHARD PIE

I'd never had much use for Swiss chard until I went to southern France, where the lively green reigns supreme, in soups, stews, side dishes, savory pies, and even desserts. Chard is particularly popular in pies, and every *boulanger* in Provence does a riff on *tourte de blette,* or Swiss chard pie—some with a flaky butter crust, some with phyllo dough, and some, like this very wonderful version, with a sturdy shell made with olive oil.

1 For the crust, put the flour in a mixing bowl, and blend in the salt with a long-tined fork. Stir in the water and the oil until a dough forms. Turn out onto a lightly floured work surface, or marble slab, and knead until the dough is smooth. Do not add more flour; the dough should be very soft.

2 Lightly butter the bottom and sides of a 10-inch tart tin (preferably the type with a bottom ring that slides out). Fit the dough into the tin, pressing it in place.

3 Heat the oven to 400°.

4 For the filling, in a small skillet, heat the olive oil. Sauté the leek until soft and translucent, about 8 minutes.

5 In another skillet, bring about an inch of water to a boil. Add the chard and season with salt and pepper. Simmer until the chard is just cooked and most of the water has evaporated, 2–3 minutes.

CRUST

1 cup unbleached flour

Pinch salt

¼ cup cool water

¼ cup extra virgin olive oil

FILLING

1 tablespoon extra virgin olive oil

1 leek, white part only, finely chopped

1 pound Swiss chard, leaves stripped from stems and chopped

Salt and freshly ground black pepper to taste

3 eggs

1 cup grated imported Parmesan cheese

¼ cup pine nuts

6 In a mixing bowl, beat together the eggs, cheese, and pine nuts. Add the leek and the chard and stir well. Pour into the pastry shell.

7 Bake about 40 minutes, until the crust is golden and a knife inserted in the center tests clean. If the top browns too quickly, lay a sheet of aluminum foil on top, and lower the oven temperature to 375°. Let cool on a rack, and serve at room temperature.

Serves 6–8

Tarte à l'Oignon

ONION TART

Rich, creamy, and slightly sweet, a comfort food like no other. If you're pressed for time, use a frozen pie shell.

1 For the filling, heat the butter and oil together in a large skillet. Add the onions, turn down the heat to low, and sauté, stirring occasionally, until the onions are soft and creamy, about 40 minutes. Meanwhile, make the crust.

2 For the crust, place the flour in a medium mixing bowl. Cut the butter or shortening into the flour, and combine by rubbing the butter or shortening and flour together with your fingers until the consistency is that of large crumbs. Add water and mix with your hands until you have a smooth dough. Transfer to a piece of greased wax paper, and refrigerate until ready to use.

3 Heat the oven to 400°. Grease a 10-inch quiche dish or an 8-inch springform pan.

4 Roll the dough over wax paper into a thin round that measures about 2 inches larger than the quiche dish or pan. Slide your hand under the wax paper and invert over the dish or pan. Turn the dough into the quiche dish or springform pan and press to fit, trimming away excess at the rim. Crimp the edges and prick the bottom with a fork. Grease a sheet of foil, and place it, greased side down, on top of the dough. Weigh down with pastry weights or dried beans. Bake for 7 minutes.

FILLING

2 tablespoons unsalted butter

1 tablespoon extra virgin olive oil

3 minced onions

CRUST

1 cup unbleached flour

5½ tablespoons unsalted butter, well chilled, or solid vegetable shortening

2 tablespoons very cold water

Pinch salt

2 large eggs

⅔ cup half-and-half

Pinch ground nutmeg

1 teaspoon salt (or to taste)

3 ounces Gruyère cheese (1 ounce thinly sliced, 2 ounces shredded)

5 Remove the crust from the oven, lift the foil and weights. Let cool before filling.

6 Turn the oven down to 375°. In a medium mixing bowl, beat together the eggs, half-and-half, nutmeg, and salt. Slowly stir in the onions.

7 Distribute sliced Gruyère over the bottom of the crust. Pour the onion mixture on top, then sprinkle evenly with shredded Gruyère.

8 Bake for 25–30 minutes, until the tart is nicely browned. Serve warm or at room temperature.

Serves 6

Torta di Spinaci
e Pignoli

A SPINACH, PIGNOLI, AND RICOTTA PIE

I love this the second day, served at room temperature.

1 For the crust, using a long-tined fork, combine the flour and salt in a large mixing bowl. Make a well in the center, and add the butter, egg, and egg yolk. With the fork or a pastry blender, combine the ingredients until crumbly.

2 Slowly add enough milk to bind the ingredients into a smooth, soft dough. Press into a ball, wrap in wax paper or plastic, and refrigerate at least 1 hour.

3 Heat the oven to 425°. Grease the bottom and sides of a 10-inch pie plate or an 8-inch deep-dish springform pan. Roll out the pastry dough to fit inside, reserving the leftover dough for the lattice.

4 Press the dough into the prepared plate or pan. Cover with foil and weigh down with pastry weights or dried beans. Be sure to distribute the weights well around the edges.

5 Bake until the crust barely starts to brown, about 6 minutes. Remove the weights and foil; let cool.

CRUST

2 cups all-purpose flour

½ teaspoon salt

1 stick unsalted butter, well chilled and cut into pieces

1 egg

1 egg yolk

3 tablespoons (approximately) milk

6 For the filling, in a mixing bowl beat together the ricotta cheese, eggs, and Parmesan cheese until well combined. Add the spinach and stir to blend. Season with salt, pepper, and nutmeg.

7 Stir in the pine nuts and raisins, and transfer to the partially baked shell. Heat the oven to 375°.

8 Cut the reserved dough into 8 strips ½-inch wide. Lay in a crosshatch pattern across the top of the pie, pinching with moistened fingers to seal on each end.

9 Bake until the filling is set and the lattice has turned golden brown, about 1 hour. If the pastry browns too quickly, cover with foil for the remaining baking time.

Serves 6–8

FILLING

Two 15-ounce containers ricotta cheese

4 eggs, beaten

½ cup grated imported Parmesan cheese

Two 8-ounce packages frozen chopped spinach, thawed and squeezed dry

Salt and freshly ground black pepper to taste

Pinch ground nutmeg

¼ cup pine nuts

¼ cup raisins

Tarte aux Champignons et Artichauts

A MUSHROOM AND ARTICHOKE PIE

I love the lively play of flavorings in this torte, which pairs rich, resonant Gruyère with the vigorous taste of dill.

1 For the crust, place the flour in a large mixing bowl and blend in the salt with a long-tined fork. Add the butter, mixing in with your fingers or a pastry blender until the consistency of crumbs.

2 Add the eggs and the lemon juice or water. Press the dough together until it binds. Turn out onto a work surface—a lightly floured board or marble slab—and work with your palms until the dough forms a smooth ball.

3 Wrap in wax paper and refrigerate for at least an hour.

4 Butter the bottom and sides of an 8-inch springform pan. Roll out the dough and fit it into the pan. Prick the bottom and sides with the tines of a fork.

5 Heat the oven to 400°. Butter a piece of aluminum foil and place it over the dough. Weigh down in place with pastry weights.

6 Bake for 10 minutes, until the dough is firm and lightly browned. Remove the weights and the foil. Return the shell to the oven and bake for 5 minutes more, taking care not to burn. Let cool before filling.

CRUST

2 cups unbleached flour

½ teaspoon salt

¼ pound unsalted butter, cut into bits

2 large eggs, lightly beaten

1 tablespoon fresh lemon juice or cold water

7 For the filling, heat the olive oil in a wide skillet. Sauté the shallots until softened, about 6 minutes. Add the mushrooms and artichokes and continue to sauté until the mushrooms are cooked through, about 8 minutes.

8 Add the wine and the spinach. Stir until the spinach turns bright green, about 2 minutes. Remove the skillet from the heat.

9 In a mixing bowl, stir together the eggs, cream, dill, and spinach mixture. Add salt and pepper. Heat the oven to 400°.

10 Distribute the Gruyère evenly over the bottom of the pastry shell. Pour the egg mixture on top. Bake for 15 minutes. Lower the heat to 375°, and bake for 20 minutes more. The torte is done when a knife inserted in the center comes out clean.

Serves 6–8

FILLING

2 tablespoons extra virgin olive oil

2 shallots, minced

6 large white mushrooms, sliced

6 frozen artichoke hearts, thawed and quartered

2 tablespoons dry white wine

10 leaves spinach, shredded

4 large eggs, lightly beaten

¼ cup cream

¼ cup minced fresh dill, or 2 tablespoons dried dill, crumbled

Salt and freshly ground black pepper to taste

4 ounces Gruyère cheese, thinly sliced

Pizza Tourte

Pizza started out in Naples, changed a bit at the hands of the Tuscans, then, well, by the time the French got hold of it, it was something else again. Something like this.

1 For the crust, using a long-tined fork, combine the flour and salt in a mixing bowl. Add the butter pieces, and, with your fingers, crumble the butter together with the flour until you've made something like coarse meal.

2 Add the water in a thin, slow stream, mixing with a fork until the dough coheres. Press the dough together into a ball, wrap in wax paper or plastic, and refrigerate at least 1 hour.

3 When ready to use, unwrap the dough, and place on a lightly floured board or a marble slab. Hit the dough a few times with a rolling pin to flatten and soften it.

4 Starting in the center of the dough, roll outward into a circle, not more than ¼ inch thick.

5 Gently lift the dough (it may help to loosen by sliding a spatula underneath), and transfer it to a 10-inch lightly buttered tart pan. Press the dough into the pan, and trim away excess dough by rolling over the top with the rolling pin.

6 Return the dough to the refrigerator for about 30 minutes.

CRUST

2½ cups all-purpose flour

¼ teaspoon salt

1 stick unsalted butter, well chilled and cut into pieces

6 tablespoons cold water

7 Heat the oven to 400°. Line the dough shell with aluminum foil. Weigh down with pastry weights or dried beans.

8 Bake at 400° for 15 minutes. Take the crust out of the oven, and remove the weights and foil. Prick the bottom of the shell with a fork, return to the oven, and bake for 3–5 minutes longer.

9 Let cool before filling.

10 For the filling, in a medium saucepan, heat the olive oil and sauté the shallot and garlic until the garlic just starts to brown. Add the dried tomatoes and stir to coat with the oil. Pour in the wine and water, and bring to a simmer. Cover, turn down the heat, and cook until the tomatoes plump and soften, about 3 minutes.

11 In a medium mixing bowl, beat together the eggs, half-and-half or milk, mozzarella, and Parmesan cheese. Pour into the prepared crust.

12 Distribute the salt, tomatoes, olives, and bell pepper evenly over the top.

13 Bake at 375° until the eggs have set and the tart has browned, about 45 minutes.

Serves 4–6

FILLING

1 tablespoon olive oil

1 shallot, minced

1 clove garlic, crushed and minced

4 sun-dried tomatoes

¼ cup dry white wine

¼ cup water

4 eggs, beaten

⅔ cup half-and-half or whole milk

4 ounces (½ cup) shredded mozzarella cheese

⅓ cup grated imported Parmesan cheese

Salt to taste

2 tablespoons pitted and minced salt-cured olives

½ small red bell pepper, roasted, peeled, and cut into thin strips (page 141)

Crepes aux Champignons et Épinard

CREPES WITH SPINACH, MUSHROOMS, AND CRÈME FRAÎCHE

If the signature smell of American public spaces is hot dogs, in much of France it's crepes. Outdoor vendors grease up their griddles with gadgets resembling paint rollers and deftly turn out soft, thin pancakes, piping hot and filled to order with creamed vegetables or jam. There are crepe bars, too, where you can order one with a glass of wine. And crepe cafés, some of which serve up so many fillings that the menus run on for several pages.

1 For the crepes, sift the flour and salt together into a mixing bowl.

2 Make a well in the center, and break the eggs into it. Whisk together until well mixed.

3 Combine ½ cup of the milk and the melted butter, and pour into the flour mixture in a slow, steady stream, whisking as you do. Continue to whisk until you have a smooth paste.

4 Whisk in the remaining milk, making a thin batter.

5 Let stand 30 minutes before frying.

6 Heat a 7-inch crepe pan. Place the tablespoon of unsalted butter in the pan, and swirl until it melts and coats the bottom of

CREPES

1 cup all-purpose flour

½ teaspoon salt

3 eggs

1 cup milk

2 tablespoons unsalted butter, melted

1 tablespoon unsalted butter

the pan. Pour the excess butter into a small dish. Reserve the excess butter for preparing additional crepes.

7 Test the pan by dropping a teaspoon of batter into it. When the batter starts hopping, the pan is ready.

8 Pour a small ladle (about ¼ cup) of batter into the pan and shake to distribute evenly. Cook over medium-high heat until the bottom has browned, about 1½ minutes. Loosen the edge of the crepe with a butter knife, then flip the crepe with your fingers. Cook until the other side has browned, about ½ minute more. Repeat for each crepe.

9 For the filling, in a medium skillet, melt the butter. Sauté the shallot until golden, but not brown. Add the mushrooms and sauté until cooked through, about 7 minutes.

10 Add the spinach and continue to cook, stirring often, until well blended. Turn off the heat and stir in the crème fraîche and Gruyère. Season with salt and pepper.

11 Place the crepes on a work surface and put the filling inside. Either roll up, tucking the ends underneath to seal, or fold the sides up like an envelope. Serve immediately. Or, if desired, place in an ovenproof dish, spoon béchamel sauce on top, and place uncovered in a 375° oven until heated through, about 3 minutes.

Makes 14–16 crepes

FILLING

1 tablespoon butter

1 shallot, minced

4 white mushrooms, thinly sliced

One 8-ounce package frozen chopped spinach, thawed and squeezed dry

2 tablespoons crème fraîche (page 25)

2 tablespoons grated Gruyère cheese

Salt and freshly ground black pepper to taste

1 cup béchamel sauce (page 24, optional)

Crepes aux Champignons

CREPES WITH MUSHROOMS

1 For the crepes, sift the flour and salt together into a bowl.

2 Make a well in the center, and break the eggs into it. Whisk together until well mixed.

3 Combine ½ cup of the milk and the melted butter, and pour into the flour mixture in a slow, steady stream, whisking as you go. Continue to whisk until you have a smooth paste.

4 Whisk in the remaining milk, making a thin batter.

5 Let stand 30 minutes before frying.

6 Heat a 7-inch crepe pan. Place the tablespoon of unsalted butter in the pan, and swirl until it melts and coats the bottom of the pan. Pour the excess butter into a small dish. Reserve the excess butter for preparing additional crepes.

7 Test the pan by dropping a teaspoon of batter into it. When the batter starts hopping, the pan is ready.

8 Pour a small ladle (about ¼) of batter into the pan and shake to distribute evenly. Cook over medium-high heat until the bottom has browned, about 1½ minutes. Loosen the edge of the crepe with a butter knife, then flip the crepe with your fingers. Cook until the other side has browned, about ½ minute more. Repeat for each crepe.

CREPES

1 cup all-purpose flour

½ teaspoon salt

3 eggs

1 cup milk

2 tablespoons unsalted butter, melted

1 tablespoon unsalted butter

FILLING

2 tablespoons unsalted butter

1 pound mushrooms, sliced

½ cup crème fraîche (page 25) or ricotta cheese

½ cup grated Gruyère cheese

Salt and freshly ground black pepper to taste

1 cup béchamel sauce (page 24, optional)

9 For the filling, in a medium skillet, melt the butter. Sauté the mushrooms until soft, about 7 minutes.

10 Using a slotted spoon or spatula, transfer the mushrooms to a mixing bowl.

11 Stir in the crème fraîche or ricotta, Gruyère, and seasonings to taste.

12 Fill each prepared crepe. Either roll it up, or fold it like an envelope. Serve immediately. Or, if desired, place in an oven-proof dish, spoon béchamel sauce on top, and heat through in a 375° oven, about 3 minutes.

Makes 14–16 crepes

Le Pezzole

FLORENTINE CREPES

Dishes called Florentine nearly always involve spinach. They were named after Florence, not by the people of that city, but by the French, whose queen, Catherine de' Medici, came from Florence and brought with her a great appetite for the green that grew so profusely outside her hometown.

1 For the crepes, sift the flour and salt together into a mixing bowl.

2 Make a well in the center, and break the eggs into it. Whisk together until well mixed.

3 Combine ½ cup of the milk and the melted butter, and pour into the flour mixture in a slow, steady stream, whisking as you go. Continue to whisk until you have a smooth paste.

4 Whisk in the remaining milk, making a thin batter.

5 Let stand 30 minutes before frying.

6 Heat a 7-inch crepe pan. Place the tablespoon of unsalted butter in the pan, and swirl until it melts and coats the bottom of the pan. Pour the excess butter into a small dish. Reserve the excess butter for additional crepes.

7 Test the pan by dropping a teaspoon of batter into it. When the batter starts hopping, the pan is ready.

CREPES

1 cup all-purpose flour

½ teaspoon salt

3 eggs

1 cup milk

2 tablespoons unsalted butter, melted

1 tablespoon unsalted butter

FILLING

1 cup ricotta cheese

Two 8-ounce packages frozen chopped spinach, thawed and squeezed dry

½ cup grated imported Parmesan

1 egg, lightly beaten

1 cup milk

Pinch ground nutmeg

1 cup béchamel sauce (page 24)

8 Pour a small ladle (about ¼ cup) of batter into the pan and shake to distribute evenly. Cook over medium-high heat until the bottom has browned, about 1½ minutes. Loosen the edge of the crepe with a butter knife, then flip the crepe with your fingers. Cook until the other side has browned, about ½ minute more. Repeat for each crepe.

9 For the filling, heat the broiler. Mix together the ricotta, spinach, Parmesan, egg, milk, and nutmeg.

10 Spread about ¼ cup of the mixture onto a crepe and roll into a cigar shape. Repeat for each crepe.

11 Put the crepes into a baking dish. Cover with béchamel, and place under the broiler until heated through, about 1 minute.

Makes 14–16 crepes

Socca / Ceicina

A CREPE OF CHICK-PEA FLOUR

The man on the train was from Nice, and, given the way he went at his lunch, I knew I could trust him to recommend a good restaurant. So I asked him where I should eat once I got there.

The marketplace, he said. Buy a slice of *socca,* a chick-pea flour crepe, which (boasting now) can be found nowhere else on earth. You must eat it with red wine, he said, and you have to eat it hot.

I found the *socca* the next day at the marketplace on Nice's Cours Salyea, spongy, spicy, scrumptious.

But then I found it again, a few weeks later, at a food stand in Siena. The Italians call it *ceicina* (from *cece,* Italian for "chick-pea"), but it's *socca,* just the same.

2 cups water

1 cup chick-pea flour (available at markets specializing in Middle Eastern foods)

4 teaspoons extra virgin olive oil

1 teaspoon fine salt

Freshly ground black pepper to taste

1 Heat the oven to 400°. Pour the water into a bowl, and mix in the chick-pea flour, 3 teaspoons of the olive oil, and the salt. Beat until smooth. Let rest 30 minutes.

2 Grease a 12-inch pizza pan or ovenproof skillet with olive oil. Pour the batter into the pan, and sprinkle the remaining 1 teaspoon olive oil over the top.

3 Bake until golden, about 10 minutes. Sprinkle generously with pepper and serve right away.

Serves 6

Fettunta

GARLIC BREAD

Not for those who prefer a faint flirtation with garlic, this *fettunta* is for the herb's most avid devotees.

1 Rub each slice of bread with the garlic.

2 Pour a thin film of olive oil into a dish large enough to hold a slice of bread. Lightly dip the bread in just long enough to sop up a bit of oil. Turn the slice over, and lightly dip the other side. (You'll probably have to replenish the oil after each slice or two.)

3 Season with salt and pepper. Serve immediately, as is, or with roasted bell peppers or Simple Tomato Sauce, if desired.

Serves 4–6

4 large slices stale Italian or French bread, lightly toasted

1 large clove garlic, split in half

Extra virgin olive oil of the best quality

Salt and freshly ground black pepper to taste

Roasted bell peppers (page 141, optional) or Simple Tomato Sauce (page 27, optional)

a few desserts

"It's not good." The waiter shook his head, wounded and sad. I had left part of my entrée on my plate, and, to a Tuscan, there could be no other explanation. "It's not good."

He was trying to commiserate, but, honestly, he had no cause. I assured him it was delicious, indeed. But so was my first course, and that was the problem. I'd eaten too much, I said. *"Non posso mangiare troppo."* ("I can't eat so much.")

He smiled wanly and cleared my plate away.

I didn't want him feeling so bad on my account, especially since I *had* enjoyed the meal. But then I saw the ricotta cheesecake, and no amount of consideration for him could stop me. I ordered dessert.

Desserts in southern France and Tuscany are, like the courses that precede them, simple and wholesome; as simple, for instance, as prunes stewed in wine, and as wholesome as semolina—known as "the flower of flours"—steamed with milk.

Crostata di Ricotta

RICOTTA CHEESECAKE

Not too sweet, and even sort of wholesome, this is, perhaps, my favorite dessert.

1 To make the crust, using a long-tined fork, combine the flour, salt, and sugar in a large mixing bowl. Work in the butter with your fingers until you've got a coarse-meal texture. Or you can combine the flour, salt, sugar, and butter in the work bowl of a food processor and process in spurts, to coarse meal.

2 If you are using a mixing bowl, beat in the egg until the dough holds together. In the food processor, incorporate the egg with short spurts, until the dough forms.

3 Turn the dough out onto a large sheet of wax paper. Press together into a ball, wrap, and refrigerate about 30 minutes.

4 Butter the bottom and sides of a deep 8-inch springform pan. Dust your fingers with flour, and press the dough into the pan. Prick the bottom of the crust with the tines of a fork.

5 To make the filling, heat the oven to 350°. With a hand mixer or food processor, beat the ricotta until smooth. Add the sugar and flour, and beat or process again until well blended.

6 Beat in the egg yolks, heavy cream, sour cream, vanilla, and lemon peel.

(continued on next page)

CRUST

1 cup all-purpose flour

Pinch salt

½ cup powdered sugar

6 tablespoons unsalted butter, well chilled and cut into pieces

1 egg, lightly beaten

FILLING

1 pound whole-milk ricotta cheese

½ cup sugar

1 tablespoon unbleached flour

4 eggs, separated, at room temperature

¼ cup heavy cream

¼ cup sour cream

1 teaspoon vanilla extract

½ teaspoon finely grated lemon zest

7 Whip the egg whites to make stiff peaks. Fold into the ricotta mixture.

8 Spoon the mixture into the prepared shell, and smooth the top with a spatula.

9 Bake the cake until the filling has set and the pastry is golden brown, 50–60 minutes. Turn off the heat. Leave the cake in the oven, with the door open, for 30 minutes. Remove and let cool at room temperature for about 2 hours before serving.

Makes one 8-inch deep-dish cake

Clafouti

Too dense for custard, too custardy for cake, clafouti defies description—although the word "delicious" does nicely, as you'll discover.

Clafouti is convenient, too; you can stir it up in no time and throw it in the oven when you sit down to dinner. When you're ready for dessert, *voilà!* dessert will be ready!

1 Sift together the flour, sugar, and vanilla powder or extract into a mixing bowl. Make a well in the center and add the eggs and egg yolks.

¼ cup all-purpose flour

⅓ cup sugar

½ teaspoon vanilla powder (see note) or extract

4 eggs

2 egg yolks

2½ cups milk

2 pounds fresh cherries, pitted

Powdered sugar

2 In a slow, steady stream, pour in 1 cup of the milk, whisking until you have a smooth paste. Whisk in the remaining milk.

3 Spread the cherries evenly over the bottom of a pie plate. Pour the batter through a strainer, over the fruit. Let sit 30 minutes.

4 Heat the oven to 375°.

5 Bake 40–45 minutes, until puffy and golden brown. Let cool 5 minutes. Sprinkle with powdered sugar and serve.

Serves 6–8

NOTE: *Vanilla powder, available in most gourmet specialty shops, has a more intense vanilla flavor than extract, which may be diluted with water or alcohol.*

VARIATIONS: *For the cherries, substitute 2 pounds of any of the following:*
- *Ripe fresh peaches, pitted, peeled, and sliced*
- *Stewed prunes*
- *Baked Fresh Figs (page 186)*

Crème Brûlée

This caramel-coated custard is ubiquitous, inevitable, you might say, in southern France.

1 Heat the oven to 400°. In a heavy saucepan, scald the cream.

2 In a mixing bowl, beat together the egg yolks and 2 table-spoons of the sugar until the yolks are thickened and a rich lemon color. In a slow steady stream, pour in the hot cream, stirring constantly. Add the vanilla.

3 Distribute the cream evenly among 4 ramekins (¾-cup capacity), or pour into a single 10-inch gratin dish. Place inside a larger baking dish, and pour cold water halfway up the sides.

4 Bake 15 minutes, until a thin film forms on the surface. (The custard *won't* be set.) Remove from the oven and refrigerate for 4 hours or overnight.

5 Just before serving, heat the broiler. Distribute the remaining sugar evenly over the top of the custard. Broil until the sugar melts into a caramel layer, about 2 minutes. Watch closely because sugar is quick to burn. Serve right away.

Serves 4–6

NOTE: *Vanilla powder, available in most gourmet specialty shops, has a more intense vanilla flavor than extract, which may be diluted with water or alcohol.*

2 cups heavy cream

5 egg yolks

½ cup fine sugar

½ teaspoon vanilla powder (see note) or extract

Mousse au Chocolat

There's a mystique around chocolate mousse, but there's really only one secret involved: The whole thing hinges on the chocolate. Great chocolate makes great mousse. You'll get better results, too, if you use a rich, aromatic blend of coffee or, better yet, espresso.

1 Heat together the chocolate and coffee in a medium saucepan. Stir until the chocolate has melted. Simmer gently until the mixture thickens slightly. Remove from the heat and beat in the egg yolks one at a time. Stir to blend well. Beat in the butter and vanilla. Set aside until tepid.

2 In a large mixing bowl, whip the egg whites to form stiff peaks. Sprinkle in the sugar and whip for another 30 seconds until the egg whites are glossy. Using a rubber spatula, fold in the chocolate. Pour into 4 individual ramekins or wineglasses. Chill for at least 4 hours.

Serves 4

6 ounces semisweet chocolate, chopped into bits

¼ cup brewed espresso or strong black coffee

4 eggs, separated

1 tablespoon unsalted butter

½ teaspoon vanilla extract

3 tablespoons sugar

Riz au Lait

RICE PUDDING

My favorite dessert in France can't be found at the famous fancy food emporium, Fauchon, or, for that matter, at any of the swank Parisian *pâtisseries*. It's called *riz au lait,* and it's sold in plastic tubs in the dairy cases at supermarkets north and south. Say I'm déclassé, but I'd rather go through a tub of *riz au lait* than a gussied-up *gâteau* any day. None of the commercial brands available in this country tastes nearly as good as the French product, but this homemade version comes close enough.

1 cup raw medium-grain white rice

4 cups milk

6 tablespoons extra-fine sugar

½ teaspoon vanilla powder (see note)

1 Fill a large saucepan with water and bring to a boil. Add the rice and boil for 2 minutes. Remove from the heat and drain off the water.

2 In another saucepan, bring the milk to a boil. Add the rice. Stir in the sugar and the vanilla powder. Bring to a simmer. Cover tightly.

3 Turn down the heat and cook until all of the milk has been absorbed, about 50 minutes. Check often after the first 35 minutes, to avoid burning.

4 Remove from the heat and let cool completely. Refrigerate overnight, and serve slightly chilled.

Serves 6–8

NOTE: *Vanilla powder, available in most gourmet specialty shops, has a more intense vanilla flavor than extract, which may be diluted with water or alcohol.*

VARIATIONS: *For a thicker pudding, after step 3 beat together 2 egg yolks, and stir 2 heaping spoonfuls of the hot rice mixture into the yolks, then stir the yolks into the rest of the rice. Continue to stir over low heat until the pudding has thickened, about 10 minutes.*

- *Substitute 1/2 teaspoon ground cinnamon for the vanilla powder.*
- *Substitute 1 teaspoon lemon zest for the vanilla powder.*
- *Stir in 1/2 cup raisins when you add the sugar.*

Semolina con Frutta / Semoule aux Fruits

SEMOLINA PUDDING

The room rate in Florence included breakfast, but I'm not miserly enough to eat what was offered for that reason alone. And there was no other reason. There were only stale rolls, suspiciously uniform slices of (processed?) cheese, and some imported muesli, which would've been fine—if not for the chocolate chips, which seemed to pervert the whole principle.

The bizarre buffet was the management's idea of what foreigners eat in the morning. Florentines don't eat breakfast; they swig espresso. If they eat anything it's likely to be a piece of soft flatbread (*focaccia*) or an almond-flavored cookie (*biscotto*). Still, I like something substantial to start my day, so I set off for the Mercato Centrale—the city's massive enclosed marketplace—and found just the thing: a fruit-flecked pudding made with semolina. Semolina is a coarsely ground wheat flour used for pasta, hot cereals, and desserts such as this.

1 Bring the milk, sugar, and vanilla to a boil. Sprinkle in the semolina or farina, stirring with a whisk. Let simmer until thickened, about 10 minutes, whisking constantly to prevent lumps.

2 Heat the oven to 375°. Lightly butter a baking dish. Beat the eggs in a bowl, and stir in the dried fruit. Whisk into the semolina mixture.

2 cups milk

½ cup sugar

½ teaspoon vanilla powder (see note)

½ cup semolina flour (you can use farina, but not instant)

2 eggs

½ cup chopped dried fruit of any kind or a combination (apples, cherries, prunes, peaches, apricots)

3 Transfer to the prepared baking dish. Place inside a larger pan, and pour water into the outer pan so that it rises halfway up the sides of the dish with the semolina.

4 Bake until the semolina mixture is firm throughout, about 40 minutes. If the top starts to brown too quickly, cover loosely with aluminum foil. Serve warm or at room temperature.

Serves 6

N O T E : *Vanilla powder, available in most gourmet specialty shops, has a more intense vanilla flavor than extract, which may be diluted with water or alcohol.*

Mascarpone Cioccolata

CHOCOLATE CREAM

Mascarpone is a soft fresh cheese that's highly perishable and often hard to find. Be relentless in your search; it's worth seeking out for use in this delicious dessert.

1 In a mixing bowl, beat together the egg yolks and sugar with an electric mixer until they become a light lemon color and ribbons form. Beat in the vanilla and cocoa.

2 Heat water in the bottom of a double boiler, and place the cocoa mixture on top. Stirring constantly, add the Kahlua a few drops at a time. Once the liqueur is incorporated, let the mixture cook for 10 minutes, stirring often.

3 Remove the cocoa mixture from the heat and let it cool thoroughly.

4 Stir in the *mascarpone*. Whip the heavy cream and fold that in, too. Distribute among 4 to 6 serving bowls and refrigerate until chilled through, about 3 hours. Serve dusted with chocolate shavings, if desired.

Serves 4–6

4 egg yolks

½ cup sugar

½ teaspoon vanilla extract

¼ cup unsweetened cocoa powder

½ cup Kahlua or other chocolate liqueur

½ pound fresh mascarpone cheese

½ cup heavy cream

2 tablespoons finely shaved semisweet chocolate (optional)

Pruneaux au Vin

PRUNES POACHED IN RED WINE

Sadly, prunes have been stigmatized for their well-known diges-
tive properties and rarely appear on American menus. Not so in
France, where stewed prunes are a justly popular dessert.

1 Soak the prunes in water to cover overnight, up to 24 hours.

2 Drain the prunes and transfer to a nonreactive saucepan, such
as enamel, with the wine, sugar, and lemon slices. Cover and
bring to a boil over high heat.

3 As soon as the mixture starts to boil, remove it from the heat.
Set aside and let cool. Serve the prunes chilled or at room temperature.

Serves 6

2 cups dried prunes

1 cup red wine

¼ cup extra-fine sugar

*2 paper-thin lemon slices
(rounds), seeded*

Figues au Four

BAKED FRESH FIGS

Serve these plain or topped with whipped cream, *mascarpone* cheese, or crème fraîche (page 25).

1 Heat the oven to 375°.

2 In a pie plate or ceramic baking dish, place enough fresh figs to cover the bottom of the dish.

3 With a long-tined fork, blend the vanilla powder with the extra-fine sugar. Sprinkle over the figs, and cover with foil.

4 Bake until soft, about 20 minutes. Serve at room temperature.

Serves 4

NOTE: *Vanilla powder, available in most gourmet specialty shops, has a more intense flavor than extract, which may be diluted with water or alcohol.*

12 large plump fresh figs

½ teaspoon vanilla powder (see note)

¼ cup extra-fine sugar

bibliographic essay

I came home from my first trip to France to find that Patricia Wells's Bistro Cooking *(Workman) had just been published. It helped me to sustain—and allowed me to share—the sensations I'd so enjoyed over there and has tided me over between trips ever since. During those trips, I've come to count on Wells's amiable, authoritative* Food Lovers Guide to France *and* Food Lovers Guide to Paris *(Workman).*

I can't say more for Mediterranean Harvest *by Paolo Scaravelli and Jon Cohen (Dutton) than that I'm on my third copy of this collection of recipes (many of them vegetarian) from Italy, France, North Africa, Greece, Turkey, and Spain. The first copy succumbed to overuse, and the second went home with a guest who'd asked to borrow it. I should have known better.*

Marielle Johnston's Cuisine of the Sun *(Fireside) has become a classic and remains (justly) the standard, not only for her infallible recipes, but for her evocative descriptions of the region. And Elizabeth David's classic* French Country Cooking *(Knopf) is still worth consulting for simple, earthy vegetable dishes.*

If not for the last word on Italian food, then for words enough to keep you engaged, informed, and very well fed, there are two books by Carol Field, The Italian Baker *and* Celebrating Italy *(both Harper and Row).*

The recipes in Cucina Fresca, Pasta Fresca, *and* Cucina Rustica, *by Viana La Place and Evan Kleiman (Morrow), are beguilingly simple and remarkably good.*

And Patience Gray's Honey from a Weed *(Harper and Row) is a perfect volume: pragmatic and poetic, a book about food—the recipes are simple—that is also an enchanting memoir of the author's years in Italy. It's informative about particulars and wise about all that can't be pinned down.*

Finally, Pino Luongo's Tuscan in the Kitchen *(Clarkson Potter) is lovely to look at and to hold in your hands. Luongo's way with recipes is truly Tuscan—he trusts you to know what you want and how best to achieve it.*

Oh, yes, and, of course, anything and everything by M. F. K. Fisher (Vintage and North Point).

index